WHAT PEOP

ESSAYS IN CONT  SM

Absolutely fascinating book, bringing together the personal thoughts and experiences of a hugely diverse group of people and their own thoughts and views on Contemporary Paganism, so many different ideas but all with a thread of commonality running through, an extremely interesting read.
Rachel Patterson, Author, *Grimoire of a Kitchen Witch*

This thought-provoking, eclectic collection of essays from Pagan writers across the globe not only gives an insight into the divergent Paganisms in various parts of the world, it also reminds us of what we – as Pagans – hold in common.
Fiona Tinker, Depute Presiding Officer, The Scottish Pagan Federation.

This anthology is like a bottle of mead and a cozy conversation with a dozen pagans round a bonfire at a summer festival, without any of the insect bites and inclement weather. I recommend it to all who want to see how we fit in to the big picture of neo-paganism around the world. It is a big YES to the question, can't we all just get along?
Dorothy Abrams, Author, *Identity and the Quartered Circle*

Essays in Contemporary Paganism

Essays in Contemporary Paganism

Edited by Trevor Greenfield

Winchester, UK
Washington, USA

First published by Moon Books, 2013
Moon Books is an imprint of John Hunt Publishing Ltd., Laurel House, Station Approach,
Alresford, Hants, SO24 9JH, UK
office1@jhpbooks.net
www.johnhuntpublishing.com
www.moon-books.net

For distributor details and how to order please visit the 'Ordering' section on our website.

Text copyright: Trevor Greenfield 2013

ISBN: 978 1 78279 278 9

A CIP catalogue record for this book is available from the British Library.

Design: Stuart Davies
www.stuartdaviesart.com

Printed in the USA by Edwards Brothers Malloy

We operate a distinctive and ethical publishing philosophy in all
areas of our business, from our global network of authors to
production and worldwide distribution.

CONTENTS

Introduction   1

1. Evolving the Spirit, Gregory Michael Brewer   2
2. Connecting Past and Future: Modern Reconstructionist
    Druidism, Morgan Daimler   12
3. A Modern Celt: The Tuatha De Danaan in the
    Twenty-First Century, Mabh Savage   23
4. Listening To the Land I Walk on, Jane Meredith   34
5. Parenting a Potentially Pagan Child, Nimue Brown   45
6. The Way of the Web: A Case Study in Online Pagan
    Experience, James Middleditch   55
7. A Week in Pagan London, Lucya Starza   66
8. A Very Modern King Arthur, Steve Andrews   77
9. Canadian Paganism – Turn and Face the North!
    Brendan Myers   87
10. Eclectic Mystic, Shirley LaBoucane   97
11. Towards a Polytheist Psychology, Robin Herne   107
12. After Paganism, Emma Restall Orr   116

Introduction

In this absorbing anthology twelve Pagan writers from across the globe offer a unique perspective on Paganism today in both its theoretical and practical aspects. Each writer began with a blank canvas, other than their essay must reflect a contemporary theme. In turn the essays are philosophical, practical, personal and reflective, with issues ranging from parenting to polytheism, from being a Pagan in London to the sacred landscapes of Australia, from mysticism to the World Wide Web. In their breadth these essays reflect a concern with living in a modern world, with modern technology and with understanding oneself within a tradition that is evolving and adapting to meet the needs of its adherents whilst staying true to its fundamental principles.

Trevor Greenfield

Evolving the Spirit

Gregory Michael Brewer

The only thing in life that is certain not to change is the fact that everything will! Pagan religion is no exception.

Contemporary Paganism is not what it was fifty years ago and will certainly be different fifty years from now. While Paganism is deeply rooted in antiquity with a rich history that can be traced back to virtually all cultures around the world via the study of mythology, surviving sacred texts, and historical documents, the true mysteries of the "Old Ways" are found only by experiencing them.

That which is now deemed Neo-Paganism, an umbrella term including Wicca, Witchcraft, Druidry, Heathenism, Asatru, Ceremonial Magick, Shamanism, Native American beliefs, Voodoo, Spiritualism, Santeria, New Age, the lost or forgotten lore of the Egyptians, Mayas, Incas, Greeks, Romans, and the list just goes on, is continuing to evolve as it always has and as it always will.

Fragments of various ancient Magickal systems, practices, beliefs, and scattered pieces of esoteric knowledge survived the Roman Catholic Inquisition, commonly referred to as the "burning times," because of the persistence and pious passion of many underground societies that preserved the knowledge within secret organizations, family traditions, and oral teachings. One may also discover many carefully preserved ancient Magickal teachings, mysteries, wisdom, and Pagan beliefs by closely examining the Bible.

A great number of Biblical stories were merely a re-telling of previously passed down Pagan legends adapted from the Egyptian, Babylonian, Sumerian, and possibly Assyrian cultures.

The ancient Biblical scribes and scholars who wrote the books of the Old Testament over a period of fifteen hundred years had been deeply influenced by and exposed to earlier Pagan theologies and myths during the enslavement of the Jews to these much older Pagan societies. A proper examination of this, however, would constitute an entire book or books.

Moving forward to the twentieth century, although it comes with some debate, Gerald Gardner's book titled *Witchcraft Today,* originally published in 1954, greatly influenced the revival of the Neo-Pagan movement by bringing Witchcraft to the light of the public eye. Many credit Gardner for resurrecting the "old religion." While Gerald Gardner did not invent Wicca, he did piece together many fragments of surviving Magickal texts and older Pagan practices. One thing that is certain, Gardner did his research, and his work was very eclectic.

Many have now deemed Gerald Gardner as "The Father of Wicca." For more information please read *Modern Wicca* by Michael Howard and *The Triumph of the Moon* by Ronald Hutton if you wish to learn about the history involved with Wicca and Gerald Gardner.

What Gardner shared with the world, along with his first and most famous High Priestess Doreen Valiente, herself the author of several books and sacred Wiccan writings including the "Charge of the Goddess," was a reconstructed fragmentary religion and practice based on Magick. This revived Magickal system gradually shifted in the late seventies and early eighties into a nature-based religion that also included Magick, and has evolved into a Pagan, or Neo-Pagan movement now counting for millions around the world.

Gardner gave birth to what have since been termed "traditions," which started with the formation of the Gardnerian tradition, followed by the Alexandrian tradition. Soon after, many other traditions of Wicca and Witchcraft were brought to the attention of the public while also giving the green light signal for older and already existent family traditions to speak up and announce their survival.

These family traditions are those that claim to have successfully endured the burning times and passed from generation to generation the ways and secrets of Magick, Paganism, and the true powers of the human mind that all too many had forgotten.

Raymond Buckland, initiated into the craft by Gardner shortly before his passing, brought Wicca to the United States and published a great many books that helped to popularize Wicca in America.

The history of Wicca and Neo-Paganism is rich and extensive, so again please read the aforementioned books if you are interested in the history of the Neo-Pagan movement.

Regardless of who founded this or that tradition, or when it all really began, one thing is certain; the reconstruction of the modern Pagan revival was going to happen regardless. There were other accounts and attempts to bring the old ways back to the public prior to Gardner, such as the works of Charles Leland, The Golden Dawn, Henry Cornelius Agrippa, Sybil Leek, Dion Fortune, Robert Graves, Margaret Murray, Laurie Cabot, George Pickingill, and a list of others too numerous to provide here.

From the late fifties to the seventies the Pagan movement, then most commonly known as, but not limited to, Witchcraft or Wicca (at that time these terms were synonymous,) brought to light even more traditions. These included Dianic groups who sought to explore the sacred feminine mysteries, Italian Witchcraft called Strega, and the reconstruction of Druidry, Asatru, and Heathenism. Again the list goes on and Paganism began to evolve into what it is today while teasing us with what it may be tomorrow.

While the current Pagan movement certainly continues to explore the mysteries and knowledge of Magick, we continue to love and embrace nature, and many, if not most, Pagans put emphasis on healing the planet and creating a personal connection with the Divine based on the archetypes of the older

Gods and Goddesses.

One thing Gerald Gardner gave to the world was a strict and specific educational training system based on the study and personal experience of the ancient Magick and Mysteries of these "Old Ways." Eventually this led to the formation of the old but sometimes still used degree system, being the First, Second, and Third degrees of Witchcraft.

It may also be relevant to point out that the traditional systems of Witchcraft that began in the late fifties were based around coven and group work, and in the late eighties and into the early nineties, Wicca saw the birth of the solitary practitioner, much credit given to the work of the late great Scott Cunningham.

Witchcraft, Wicca, and the Pagan movement at large is once again evolving and changing.

While some may not like to hear it, the older traditions are slowly being tossed to the wayside and the rise of the eclectic Witch, Wiccan, and Pagan is on the forefront.

Eclectic Wicca, Witchcraft, and Paganism may seem to some a move to make legitimate a "watered down" version of older practice and study, but nothing could be further from the truth.

The eclectic evolution of Paganism brings to the cauldron a rich and wonderful supply of knowledge and Magickal techniques that stand to enrich and empower the practitioner, such as Shamanism and Eastern teachings including Reiki and the study of the aura and Chakra system, while still keeping the heart of the older traditions alive. For this reason Paganism today is worthy of being called a "living religion."

What is a living religion? A living religion is a religion, faith, or spirituality that constantly grows, changes, and evolves over time just like a tree slowly grows new boughs, branches, and leaves each year that reach higher and higher toward the sun. A living religion has no set-in-stone doctrine or dogma; it changes and evolves over time. A living religion does not claim to have the only true and right way, but understands that the Divine can be experienced by all regardless of his or her personal path and is tolerant of all spiritual beliefs and paths.

Paganism is indeed a living religion and will continue to change and evolve into the future just as it has historically done in the past.

I have studied and practiced Witchcraft, Wicca, and Paganism in general for twenty years. During that time I have gone back and forth between small group practice, solitary study, large group participation, and the latter is where I choose to remain, for in my opinion there is no greater joy than to teach others, learn from others, and to celebrate together. Participating in a group environment and experiencing the mysteries from other perspectives is often greater than reading about them in a book (although books are quite beneficial and a valuable resource of knowledge), or experiencing them on an individual quest, because love, laughter, and tolerance are provided within the structure of the group mind.

There is a time and calling for solitary practice and a time to join a group or find a teacher, but lest we forget the greatest mystery and Magick of all, which is love, forgiveness, and acceptance of not only others but also of ourselves, we must learn to work together regardless of traditions and be not only tolerant of other paths, but to learn from and support each of them.

In addition I currently serve on the Council of Elders for the Circle of the Spirit Tree, a Wiccan study group/coven, and coordinate the Chicago Pagan Pride event while also serving as the Regional Coordinator of the Upper Midwest Region for the Pagan Pride Project Worldwide, a 501 c3 tax-exempt not-for-profit entity that supports events in almost every state in the U.S.A, Central and South America, Europe, and Australia.

The Pagan Pride Project attempts to not only provide a day for Pagans in the area to come and celebrate together, but to invite the public to each local event in order to debunk the myths that

Pagans have had to deal with for far too long. We also provide food for the homeless in local communities and offer public rituals. This is another example of how Paganism is changing and evolving.

In the time of my own study and practice, I have seen many changes, all for the better in my opinion, regarding the direction of Paganism.

Years ago I worked with colleagues of mine to begin the creation of our group's (The Circle of the Spirit Tree) educational system. Even to this day we still add an occasional lesson or revise an older one, but our initial goal was, and still is, to teach and guide those who feel the need to belong to a group and those who wish to learn the ways of Magick and experience the mysteries of the Divine.

We have set up our very eclectic education system so that whether one is a complete beginner or an adept, there is something to learn and something to teach.

The traditional First, Second, and Third degree system was just not enough to teach and share everything involved with Paganism and the ways of Magick today, but we still use a blueprint of this older system while expanding on it to include as much knowledge as possible for those who wish to learn.

For example, what our group calls Initiate Degree is based on a "traditional" approach to First Degree and teaches the basics of Pagan history – specifically of the Wiccan religion – and Magick, in other words, Wicca 101.

We have split Second Degree into four additional degrees being Earth Degree, Air Degree, Fire Degree, and Water Degree and each lesson builds upon the others. During the time of each elemental degree the seeker/student is able to make a personal bond and connection with each element.

After completing Water Degree the devoted student is able to initiate into the Third Degree of the High Priesthood.

In addition we teach nature and survival skills in each of the sub-degrees, such as learning to identify and understand the medicinal/Magickal properties of the trees and other herbs for Earth Degree while also including how to communicate with animal totems, spirit guides, advanced divination techniques, how to cook with Magick, and hands-on Magickal exercises to connect with the land.

In Air Degree we teach how to identify the stars and encourage memorization and reading, to name just a few skills. Fire Degree requires one to be able to build a fire from scratch and properly extinguish it with a true understanding of how to control one's own fires and passions. Water Degree students must be able to create various potions and elixirs to heal or banish negativity. Ultimately, each who reaches this level of study is required to control their emotions and face his or her "Shadow Self" in order to begin learning how to accept and improve personal faults, use constructive criticism, and transform the baneful into beauty. This is the real alchemical process of turning lead to gold. There is much more to it of course and it usually takes three or four years to get though the basic degrees. The important thing to know is that we also include the aspects of religion, mythology, and Magick that have been passed down and shared around the world and not limited to Wicca and Neo-Paganism alone.

Our group is not the first, nor will it be the last, to include an expanded education system that lives up to the true meaning of the term "eclectic."

The shift to eclecticism, however, seems to be taking hold all over the global Pagan spectrum.

The well-known author and Witch Janet Farrar, who now writes and works with Gavin Bone, recently wrote and published a book titled *Progressive Witchcraft*. While Janet was initiated into the Alexandrian tradition in the seventies under Alex Sanders himself, and practiced with the late great Stewart Farrar, she continues to contribute to the evolution of Paganism and

Witchcraft. When I read *Progressive Witchcraft* it felt as though Janet was talking about our own group because she and Gavin spoke of the degree system of educating based on the elements and seems to support the evolution of the eclectic Witch, Pagan, and Magickal practitioner.

The best-selling author Christopher Penczak, who has written over seventeen books on the topic of Witchcraft, also uses an elemental based educational training system. Again the list goes on and we can see Paganism/Witchcraft as evolving and embracing an eclectic approach.

While I cannot claim to know what Paganism will be tomorrow, I can see the direction it is heading, and more of an eclectic evolutionary inclusion will transpire, for it must do in order to remain a living religion.

Just as the "ancients" were not ancient in their time, so we will be the ancients of tomorrow, and although our ancestors before the domination of Catholicism and Christianity did not call themselves Pagan, they certainly shared the mythology and Magickal systems of their surrounding communities with each other.

Paganism has always been eclectic, will always be eclectic, and will always continue to evolve. If you are like me, and so many others who have a hard time with change, there is comfort in knowing that things will never change so long as you know they always will.

Let us evolve with Spirit and let us allow Spirit to evolve us.

Now don't be disappointed, I have a bit more to share. I knew you would be excited! Below I am sharing with you an exercise to experience the Magick and mysteries on your own and a way to attune yourself with the elements and the Divine.

Following this is an atonement exercise and not a complete ritual, although it could be incorporated into one if so desired. For this exercise there is no need to cast a circle, but please do so if you feel the need, and if you are able to do this outdoors, even better it will be, but not necessary by any means.

Magickal Exercise

Stand and face the East.

Visualize a yellow mist or light surrounding you.

Repeat out loud the following or re-write something similar in
    your own words:

Good evening/morning/afternoon spirits of the East and Air.

I am the spirit of the wind.

I am the song and dance of the birds.

I am the essence of thought and intellect.

I speak, I listen, I teach, and I learn.

My spirit spreads its wings and soars to other realms and back
    again.

Allow the energy of Air to blow into you.

Face the South.

Visualize a red mist or light surrounding you and repeat:

Good evening/morning/afternoon spirits of the South and Fire.

I am the essence of passion, change, and transformation.

I am the master of my own will.

I am in tune with the God and the sun.

I am a light to those around me as I heal, inspire, and glow.

My flames safely reach out and grow higher and higher.

I harm no others.

Let the Fire of passion and transformation ignite within you.

Face the West.

Visualize a blue mist or light surrounding you and repeat:

Good evening/morning/afternoon spirits of the West and Water.

I am the embodiment of emotion and the depths of the ocean.

My intuition and psychic abilities safely open and grow stronger
    everyday!

I am in tune with the Goddess and the Moon.

I feel, I understand, I love, and I forgive.

Let the Waters of Magick flow within you.

Face the North.

Visualize a green light or mist surrounding you and repeat:

Good evening/morning/afternoon spirits of the North and Earth.

I am stable, I am completely healthy on all levels, and I am a rock of success and the cave of secrets.

I have all the money that I need and I have plenty extra to give.

My ability to heal others and myself is now safely opening and growing.

I am one with the stones, the trees, the plants, and the mountains.

Allow the energies of Earth to ground and empower you.

Move into the center of the working area and raise your hands up high.

Visualize a white light or mist flowing into you and surrounding you. Repeat:

Good evening/afternoon/morning spirit of the Spirit.

I give thanks for all that I have ever had, all that I do have, and all that I will have.

I am your child (speak mundane or Magickal name.)

I AM in control of my life and I AM the creator of my own universe!

I AM the perfect balance and an inspiration to others.

Fill me with your light, your power, and your Magick.

Guide and protect me always.

Allow the mysteries of the Divine and the balance of the Masculine and Feminine aspects of the universe to be one with you and the fabric of your very existence.

Say loudly with authority: *"So Mote It Be!"*

Only by experiencing hands-on the mysteries and Magick of Spirit are we able to embrace the evolution of Spirit and understand that Paganism is and has always been a living religion that embraces all and reaches higher and higher to our future destination.

Blessed Be.

Connecting Past and Future:
Modern Reconstructionist Druidism

Morgan Daimler

Celtic polytheism and Druidism are both flourishing in the modern world in a variety of different ways. Celtic polytheism, the worship of Celtic deities, can be found in many different neopagan paths, from Celtic-oriented Wicca, which is modern Wicca that honors Celtic gods, to Celtic reconstructionism, which is the worship of Celtic gods based on historical research and cultural context. In the same way Druidism is seen in many expressions, from the purely philosophical approaches to the neopagan religious ones; many groups exist for each of these many approaches. Out of all these myriad approaches to Celtic polytheism perhaps the most unusual, and sometimes controversial, is reconstructionist Druidism, the melding of neopagan Druidism and a reconstructionist approach to practice. Reconstructionist Druidism may best be described as the way that some people are seeking a viable, spiritually enriching, modern path that is strongly rooted in the beliefs and practices of our ancestors through the synthesis of reconstruction and neopagan Druidism.

Modern Druidism was born during the Druidic revival of the 1700s when the Druids went from a subject of study in England to a motivator for the formation of groups. These early groups were fraternal or charitable orders and were decidedly Christian. In the 1940s, as modern paganism began to gain momentum, some revivalist Druid groups began to move away from the older models, and within thirty years modern neopagan Druidism had begun to take root. In America this was first expressed by the Reformed Druids of North America and later by a wide array of groups including Ar nDraoicht Fein (ADF) and the Henge of

Keltria. As these groups were gaining ground and followers a new movement began which rejected overtly neopagan concepts and instead embraced a paganism based on researching and re-envisioning historic paganism; this movement would eventually coalesce into Celtic Reconstructionism. By the late 1990s some Druidic groups, such as the Order of the White Oak, had begun to synthesize the two, looking for ways to practice modern Druidism based on as much historical material as possible.

Reconstructionist Druids face challenges from Revivalist and neopagan Druids as well as practitioners of Celtic reconstructionism. Many Revivalist Druids view Druidry as a philosophy or way of life rather than as a religion, which is sharply at odds with the reconstructionist Druids view of Druidism as a modern expression of Celtic paganism. The terms used to describe the religion reflect this with philosophical Druids tending to favor the word "Druidry" and religious Druids sometimes favoring "Druidism". Even among the religious Druids differences can be found; while neopagan Druids may see what they do as a religion, they may not be specifically Celtic, usually a key factor for reconstructionist Druids, and they may also freely incorporate modern or foreign concepts that reconstructionist Druids reject. This can create tension between Druids with different approaches or viewpoints. In the same way Celtic reconstructionists tend to view Druids not as a religion on their own but as the priestly class of the pagan Celts; many Celtic reconstructionists reject the idea of any modern Druid completely, or else have very strict criteria that must be met which often would exclude almost all modern Druids. This places reconstructionist Druids in something of a no-man's-land between the two larger groups. Despite these challenges many modern Druids are being drawn to a reconstructionist approach and reconstructionist Druidism seems to be gaining popularity.

Reconstructionist Druids often focus on one specific Celtic culture, such as Irish or Welsh, and base their beliefs and practices on the study of the historic paganism of those cultures as well as the modern cultures themselves. An Irish reconstructionist Druid, for example, would rely on scholarship, mythology, history, archeology and anthropology of the pagan Irish but would also incorporate modern folklore and cultural practices. This follows the idea that true reconstruction is not about recreating a single moment in history, but rather is about imagining what that pagan culture would have been today if it had never been subsumed by another religion or culture. A part of this is understanding the modern culture; many reconstructionist Druids actively participate in different aspects of the culture they connect to including listening to the music, cooking the food, and speaking or appreciating the language. Although it is not at all necessary for a person to have any ancestry within the culture they are spiritually drawn to, many reconstructionist Druids do have this connection to their culture and so may have been raised in it or else see continuing the cultural traditions as a way to honor their ancestors.

There is as much variety within reconstructionist Druidism as there is in the wider context of general Druidism and so making any generalized statements must come with the acknowledgement of the inevitable exceptions to anything that is said. However, it is possible to discuss reconstructionist Druidism in general terms by taking the wide view of the most common beliefs and practices. Most reconstructionist Druids agree with the Celtic reconstructionist view of Druids as ritual leaders, magic workers, and the general educated class of the historic Celts. What is known about the ancient Druids from historic sources such as the Greek and Roman writers, as well as from mythology, shows a class of professionals who fostered with a senior Druid at an early age and trained for many years to learn the needed skills. Druids were advisors to leaders, healers, lawyers, diviners, and acted as the mediators between the people and the gods. For those that follow reconstructionist Druidism understanding who the historic Druids were is very important to integrating the past with the present. Many such Druids look for ways to nurture those qualities and skills that the ancient Druids were known for within themselves, in order to truly be a Druid in the modern world. Others do not call themselves Druids at all but consider themselves to be on the spiritual path of a Druid. All seem to seek to serve their communities in the best ways they can, and to serve the Gods and Spirits.

Generally reconstructionist Druids honor the Gods, spirits of the land and Otherworld, as well as the ancestors. Within reconstructionist Druidism there are many different views and opinions on the nature of the Gods but there is a rough consensus in favor of polytheism; whether the Gods are seen as deified ancestors or Beings separate from humanity they are viewed as uniquely individual, as opposed to the more common neopagan views of gods as archetypes or aspects of a single Power or pair of Powers. Some people have adopted a way of looking at all beings on scales of power, with Gods at the highest end, humans at the other end and ancestral spirits and land spirits or fairies ranging in-between. This can be one way to interpret the concept found in the Irish of the "Gods and non-gods", although it is by no means the only way to understand the concept. Honoring ancestors, Otherworldly spirits and Gods is a reciprocal process through which offerings are given and blessings received, creating a relationship between the people and the spirits. Reconstructionist Druids may focus more or less on any of these three types of beings depending on their own personal beliefs and focuses. For some a balance between all three is sought, while others may focus heavily on one or two out of the three.

One of the initial challenges to a reconstructionist approach of any type is source material for understanding the Gods and Otherworldly spirits, and this is particularly true of those seeking a Celtic path. Since the pagan Celts themselves did not record any of their own beliefs or stories we are left with secondary sources and mythology recorded during the Christian period. Although this material is biased in different ways it still has great value for anyone with the patience to comb through it. An Irish or Welsh reconstructionist can create a fairly complex picture of their Gods using these sources and gain a good understanding of the beliefs surrounding Otherworldly beings the same way. Those interested in Gaul and other areas for which less material survived will have a more difficult time but can still create a workable understanding of a religious framework. This understanding is essential to a reconstructionist approach, which seeks to rebuild the lost paganism of a certain culture rather than create something new; for a reconstructionist Druid who is seeking to, effectively, not only reconstruct Celtic paganism but also to modernize and fill the role once held by the ancient Druids, understanding the Gods is vital. One cannot act as an intercessor between people and the Gods, whether by making offerings or divination, without first having that connection to the Gods themselves.

For those that seek to also connect to the uniquely Celtic understanding of the beings of the Otherworld, sometimes called aes sidhe or faeries, the best possible source is the Fairy Faith. Although the Fairy Faith itself has been heavily influenced by Christianity over the centuries it is still the best and most in-depth repository of not only beliefs but also practices relating to the subject. Studying and understanding the historic views and approaches to dealing with the Otherworld through this lens can provide a solid foundation to build a modern Druidic practice that stays true to the Celtic viewpoint. Careful reading of the mythology can also add layers of understanding which are important to anyone seeking genuine connection. Many of the modern ideas about faeries are sharply at odds with the traditional view, sometimes in ways that are not at all compatible. For any modern pagan this subject is muddied by the sheer number of books now on the market that are written from this new and, to a reconstructionist, utterly foreign viewpoint.

Honoring our ancestors is also an important aspect of reconstructionist Druidism. As with anything else in the religion there is a great deal of variance in how anyone chooses to approach this. For some it means connecting to personal ancestors, while to others it may also include honoring collective or cultural ancestors. Ancestor veneration may be expressed with simple words and small offerings or with a complex shrine or altar that might include pictures of deceased family members. Lighting candles is one way to honor those who have passed and people who follow specific cultures might include the practices of those cultures relating to the dead, such as the Irish practices around Samhain.

The view of cosmology may vary slightly depending on the particular culture a person works in, but overall there are common themes. The number three is emphasized and can be seen from the variety of triple deities to the use of wisdom sayings called "triads". The importance of three can also be seen in the view of the world as consisting of three realms, sea, earth, and sky. We are told that Celtic warriors would swear an oath by these three, asking that if they broke their word the sea should rise up and drown them, the earth should open and swallow them and the sky should fall on them. Many modern groups expand on this idea of three realms to form a basic cosmology. To this is often added fire as a symbol of inspiration and life, sometimes called imbas (Old Irish) or awen (Welsh). The historic Celts did not and most reconstructionist Druids do not use the classical four element system; rather a complex system was used that could include nine or more elements. Within a ritual setting many do not acknowledge different directions or elemental correspondences although some do choose to do so using a system based either on the story of the Settling of the Manor of Tara or the myth of the four cities of the Tuatha de Danann.

Similarly some will argue that all space is sacred and that creating sacred space is therefore redundant, while others believe that space for ritual should be chosen based on natural "sacredness" of the place, and others believe that it is important to bless or consecrate a space for ritual use. On this issue there seems to be the least amount of agreement.

The ancient Celts have no known creation or eschatology stories, although it is unknown if the cultures actually lacked them or if they simply did not survive to the modern era. For reconstructionist Druids the choice becomes to either borrow in such stories from closely related cultures, such as the Norse, to create new stories based on a study of Indo-European cultures, or to ignore the gaps created by their lack. Since these stories are important but not vital to the practice of the spirituality there is no single option which is better or worse than the others. It becomes a matter of personal choice and how much weight an individual gives to their value.

The view on holidays depends on which culture the person or group is reconstructing as well as how strongly reconstructionist they are trying to be. At one end of the spectrum are the reconstructionist Druids who will only celebrate verifiable ancient holidays; from an Irish perspective these would be Imbolc, Bealtaine, Lughnasa, and Samhain, although even Imbolc is sometimes questioned as lacking mythological and historic references. Others will celebrate these four, often referred to as the "fire festivals", as well as the equinoxes and solstices, while at the far opposite end of the spectrum are those who include these eight as well as additional modern holidays, such as those to honor certain heroes or historic figures. Even for those who celebrate the same set of holidays as each other the actual celebrations can be different as people choose to incorporate or ignore different historical practices in recreating the modern practices. Even choosing the dates to celebrate can vary between people and groups as some use agricultural markers while others use calendar dates and still others use astronomy. For example within Irish reconstructionist Druids celebrating Samhain one might use the date of the first frost, a second might use the modern calendar date of Halloween, and a third might wait until Scorpio is at 7 degrees. Acknowledging these holidays, in one combination or another, is also common to Celtic reconstructionists and to different neopagans; the reconstructionist Druid perspective on seasonal holidays tends to be closer to the Celtic reconstructionist views in that the celebrations themselves are usually based on historic precedent and folk practice.

Reconstructionist Druids also usually incorporate honoring or acknowledging certain phases of the moon, based on references in secondary sources of the ancient Druids doing so. This is particularly true of the new moon, or the first sliver of crescent visible after the dark moon, although again the timing varies between groups. Many also choose to honor the full moon, based on the references to doing so found in sources such as the Carmina Gadelica. The existence of folk practices and charms that honor the full moon supports the idea of modern reconstructionist Druids doing so. Usually these rituals are designed around and focused on fragments of belief and surviving prayers that can be found within the individual Celtic cultures.

Ritual tools are not often discussed or emphasized in Celtic reconstruction, yet play a significant role in other types of neopaganism. Many reconstructionist Druids do choose to use ritual tools, although they choose to look to history for an understanding of what the ancient Celts may have used in ritual. Each different group and practitioner may come to different conclusions about what should be used and why, but in general Druidic tools mentioned in mythology can be commonly seen. Wands and staffs tend be more common, as well as cauldrons. Many people choose to incorporate symbolism relating to Celtic cosmology within their altar space, and most will also include something to hold offerings. Images of deities may or may not be found as it is known that the Celts, in at least one instance when sacking Rome, commented on the foolishness of depicting Deities in material form. Clearly this changed later as there are images in Gaul, albeit influenced by Roman occupation.

Ritual itself can be either complex or simple depending on the person's approach to it. There are a few points, though, that most if not all reconstructionist Druids include in ritual. Most rituals start with some acknowledgement of the gods and spirits which will include offerings of some sort. The body of the ritual itself usually includes prayers and a specific offering for the occasion or the main deity of the rite. The emphasis on offerings comes from the historic evidence that offerings formed the backbone of Celtic religion; this can be seen in the large deposits of gold and silver given as votive offerings that the Romans discuss in several sources, as well as the discovery by archeologists of a variety of different votive deposits at shrines in Celtic countries. Beyond this many rituals also include the inclusion of or acknowledgement of the three realms discussed earlier.

Magic is also often an integral part of reconstructionist Druidism although its presence may be very subtle. There is a great deal of evidence relating to the Druids using magic in mythology and secondary sources, especially relating to battle magic, healing, and divination. We see Druids such as Fedelm and Cathbad prophesying about important events, for example, and there is strong evidence surrounding the Druidic use of certain types of prophecy methods called imbas forosnai, teinm liada, and dichetal do chennaib in Irish myth. This lays the foundation for a modern use of these practices by Druids, although in many cases the information about the actual methodology is limited and must be expanded on. Similarly the understanding of other types of Druidic magic tend to be limited to descriptions of the results rather than the actual practices used so that a modern practitioner is left to guess and experiment to achieve the desired results. In many cases reconstructionist

Druids who are interested in healing focus on learning about herbal medicine, but may be as knowledgeable about the folkloric magical uses of an herb as the practical medical uses. For some people the study of Druidic magic, often done through the study of folk customs and beliefs as well as mythology, may be a main aspect of their practice, while others may never go beyond basic blessings and divinations.

Reconstructionist Druids, like many other types of pagans, are animists who see spirits in all things, but this path tends to emphasize connecting to nature and the natural world as well as simply acknowledging that awareness of spirit. Celtic myth is full of stories of the spirits of place personified as animals or human-like beings and some reconstructionist Druids connect to modern spirits of place this way while others may only relate to feeling different kinds of energy. Many modern Druids are very environmentally aware, although environmentalism is more a by-product of the religion than a core belief. We do know that the ancient Druids worshipped in sacred groves and held certain types of trees as especially meaningful or powerful, and this can carry over to modern reconstructionist Druidism through a concern for the world around us and an emphasis on using these same types of places and materials.

All of this combined, touches on the basics of belief and ritual within reconstructionist Druidism, but this is only a small part of the actual spiritual path. In day to day practice the path is also about living an honorable life, seeking Truth, and connecting to the world around us and the various spirits within it. Many use daily devotionals to help intertwine their spirituality and their daily lives in the most effective way, and may study Celtic myth and folklore daily looking for ways to relate the old to the new. Reconstructionist Druids are raising children within their own religion and looking at the ways that children and a new gener-ation of Druids can be taught; for some this is through living what they believe while others take a more active teaching approach but all seem to view their religion as inclusive of children. Reconstructionist Druidism is, at its heart, something that includes family and community, even in situations where the family and community are not themselves Celtic pagans. The qualities and beliefs of a reconstructionist Druid touch every aspect of the person's life in ways that will also inevitably affect the people around that individual. Being a Druid of any type is not about taking on a certain role for a few hours at certain times of year, but rather about making that role a part of who you are all the time, so that it is an inseparable part of your identity.

In the end reconstructionist Druidism in many ways is a melding of the strengths of Celtic reconstructionism and neopagan Druidism, with its emphasis on genuine spiritual connection and service to the community combined with its focus on academic research and historical precedent. It represents the melding of two spiritualities that often reject each other into a cohesive whole that offers a viable religion to those who cannot find a place in either mainstream modern Druidism or Celtic reconstructionism without feeling conflicted. Undoubtedly it will continue to be a controversial approach to Celtic spirituality, just as the people within the practice of reconstructionist Druidism continue to struggle to define their own methods and beliefs. In many ways this approach to spirituality is still in its infancy, yet it is strong and continues to attract people willing to invest the time and effort to move it forward.

A Modern Celt: The Tuatha De Danaan in the Twenty-First Century

Mabh Savage

I never really referred to myself as a pagan until I was in my early twenties. I always thought of myself as a witch, and I guess even with this I had my own definition. I know some people shy away from using the word witch because of its many negative connotations, but seeing as it wasn't really something I discussed with, well, anyone, it didn't seem to matter. Meeting other like-minded, or similar minded people led me into the somewhat dubious habit of referring to myself as a Pagan, simply to help others pigeon hole me. I'm not sure I actually fit the current definition of Pagan, seeing as most definitions you find will refer to the religious aspects of the term, and I do not think of myself as religious at all. If you go to any Pagan gathering and ask ten different people what being a Pagan means to them, you will most likely get ten completely different answers! But I do practice witchcraft; I do follow the Celtic wheel of the year and celebrate the festivals accordingly, so because many Pagans do this I guess I fall into that bracket. So why, here, do I refer to myself as a Celt? A modern Celt? Really that's an oxymoron, as the term Celt is a point of historical reference for a people that no longer exist as such. What I'm referring to are the aspects of the Celtic world that have survived into the twenty-first century including the wheel of the year and the stories and legends of their gods and spirits, including the Tuatha De Danaan.

I literally was astounded when I found out that the first (and only real) group I had the chance to work with, honoured the Morrigan. Wow, here was a figure from mythology, a goddess and a legend who I had been fascinated with since I was a tiny girl: a monster in the books of Alan Garner; a sorceress in the songs of Horslips (check out The Tain by Horslips - amazing). A woman with so many faces; from monster to maid; warrior to crone; a part of my heritage and a key player in the Tuatha De Danaan. I had always been taught these beings were a huge part of my Celtic roots, and here I was, apparently by chance, in a group of people who had made her their focus for all things magical. I had spent a great many years at this point being cynical and doubtful of many things I had previously taken for granted, such as the presence of any sort of energy one may refer to as fate, or destiny, or the idea of being on a path where one is supposed to be. This single incident alone pushed me closer to the idea of external forces guiding us than probably any other event in the last ten years. It was as if someone had said, ok, you wanna know about your Celtic roots? Well let's introduce you to one of them and see what happens!

There were other astounding discoveries to be made that I can't go into in too much detail for fear of breaking vows of privacy and bonds of friendship - a story told in confidence is a powerful binding! But let it just be said that I have been fortunate enough to discover that it's not just me that longs to open a window into these fantastic stories, legends, and whatever else one may name the Tuatha De Danaan.

So, how exactly does one do this? And how do they, as deities or spirits, lend themselves to magical workings? Well firstly, I better explain what I mean by this. If you're reading this then hopefully you've got a vague idea that some Pagans practice magic. Not all and some will not refer to it as that, so please forgive me if I generalise. "What is magic?" is yet another question, like the aforementioned "What is a Pagan?" that gives multiple answers, all correct, all unique to the person you are asking and probably all contradictory to some extent! My own understanding is that magic is the science and understanding of the way things work. What things you ask? Everything! When a tulip starts sprouting in the snow, aware of the warm months ahead, this is magic. When the bus comes literally as I get to the stop, that's magic too. When I don't get a role at work that I wanted so have more time to work towards a different endeavour, this is also magic. "That's not magic, that's just things happening! Normal things!" I hear you cry. Oh yes. Magic is normal. Magic is everyday events. Magic is the world changing around us, just outside our control but close enough to appear mundane. My definition of *practicing* magic, using it as a tool, is that you move that little bit closer to the world and you *take control*. It's a very human thing and some people do it without any conscious effort. Those who always get the job they want, or win £10 on scratch cards weekly; you all know someone like this: an individual who seems incessantly lucky.

I think it works the other way too; I'm sure that those people who always seem down on their luck and always seem to be carrying burdens or personal tragedy; I think perhaps they are also closely connected to the world but for whatever reason they attract the wrong sort of events. I have no idea how this works, it's just an approximate theory, and a hair's breadth away from total digression so let's continue on ...

To summarise, when you do a magical working, you have a goal in mind (hopefully!) and you do something in order to make it happen, to in fact, partially or completely take control of events. Sometimes this may be as simple as wanting to feel a connection to something; a god, a spirit, the energy involved with the change of season. I refer to this practice as witchcraft, and in this bracket I include herbalism, making incense, writing music (powerful music anyway, music that moves someone in some way) and pretty much anything that involves changing the world in some way, however small. Most witches I have met deal primarily with people, and usually practice healing of some sort. There's no way to say "how" to do this without giving a context because literally everyone will do things differently; I know people who will spend days working with a specific deity to help someone through a time of illness, and others who seem to be able to reassure and bolster another's spirit with but a thought. So we return to the question; how do the Tuatha De Danaan lend themselves to magical workings, to witchcraft - how can these Celtic legends, these deities or spirits that have survived millennia, be relevant today?

Interestingly my first direct working within the group I fell in with was not actually focusing on Morrigan, but on the goddess Brigid. The name of many pronunciations! Even in a ritual setting I have heard her name perhaps pronounced three different ways, but indeed it does seem that she has had many incarnations over the years so perhaps this is appropriate. St Brigid is a possible Christianisation of this triple goddess of spring, and it's not a huge jump to see links to Persephone in her legend too. Here is an Irish goddess who tells a very human story. She works with smiths, bards and farmers; festivals for her bring communities together in anticipation of the coming spring and defeat of winter; celebration of the fertility of the land and indeed of the young women who dance in her honour; dolls are made and fires are burned all to show that the human spirit is not only surviving but thriving. Her story tells that as the daughter of the Dagda, she was born at daybreak, rising into the sky with fire burning in her hand, spreading sunlight across the land. Later in her tale she marries Bres of the Fomorians, hoping to achieve unity and a peace between the two peoples. Her sons are great warriors, and when one dies on the battlefield it is Brigid's grief stricken keening that prevents further bloodshed.

What's the relevance of these stories in this modern age? How can we possibly relate to a world of human gods and goddesses, tribal disputes and deep, dark magic? Well I guess there's a touch of sarcasm there as the sentence kind of answers itself; we all aspire to be something greater than we are, everyone; the idea of gods and goddesses not as distant, unreachable enigmas, but as real, emotional, flesh and blood and above all flawed beings is very attractive - not something to live up to, but something to allow us to examine and judge ourselves. The world is constantly torn by war and especially civil unrest, as seen so often on the news lately, so the stories of the warring Celtic tribes and the Book of Invasions (the "history" of the many tribes that invaded Ireland) seem to have a particular poignancy right now. And as we are in a Pagan anthology here, how can we not be interested in magic and mysticism; fantastic worlds of things just beyond the mind's eye? The lure of the Tuatha de Danaan is in the combination of fantasy and reality; astonishing magical creatures caught in very human situations; war, love, sex and death. Each story can be a metaphor for something in your life, each being a personification of an attribute you may, or may not, want to bring into focus in your life.

For example, when I think of anger, I imagine the Morrigan, fierce and terrible, but using that energy to do what she thinks is the right thing to do; not, and this is important, necessarily the moral thing! But what seems like the best choice at the time. So yes, be angry, but don't dither, don't wail, focus that anger and turn it into productivity, thereby harnessing the power of that emotion. The story becomes a way to set yourself right, to literally have a word with yourself and stop yourself drifting into destructive behaviour. There are other ways to harness the magic within the Tuatha de Danaan; I occasionally appeal to the Morrigan for dreams to guide me, and this is often hard and the dreams can be terrible and nightmarish, yet I feel that this is the influence of a being, a force if you will, that has been associated with war and death for so long that she cannot help but bring these shadows with her, and you have to look beyond this to find the message. Often this is something I already know, and the message is from within me - the dream has simply helped me contextualise and understand this. I leave her offerings of mead and wine, always something I would have myself and enjoy. Her space is given over to very personal or purely natural items; a flat stone holds incense; a shell symbolises water; a brush from my great grandmother symbolises the connection to my ancestors, my roots; a malachite crystal ball hints to her powers of prophecy, and the deep swirling green of it speaks to me of earth, and hidden mysteries.

These are all items that say something about me, but make me think of her, of mystery, of my Celtic roots and the day to day life that often is interspersed with magical interludes. For I do not believe that magic only comes when you call it, but is around us all the time, causing change and wonder for any that care to see or experience it. Right now I can walk to the end of the ginnel at the back of my house, and stand by a deep hawthorn hedge, inhaling spring rain while my ears fill with the waterfall of birdsong from the robins and blackbirds that rustle gently through the green. Brambles creep around me while cats watch from dripping wooden fences, stony skies close and wet, heavy with the promise of a storm. Cool air raising each hair on my arms, flattening my coat against my chest while my shoes sink slightly in the sodden soil, rooting me in place. Suspended in a web of being, a tiny speck of life in an endless universe; this is magical, wondrous, not grasping at understanding but accepting existence as a fact and a gift.

This feeling of being a part of the world, not just something walking upon it, is what lets us feel the changes as winter gives way to spring, and spring bursts into summer. The Celtic year is all about taking notice of the seasons, understandable when you realise that this originates from a time when not paying attention to the turning weather could mean planting food at the wrong times, a ruined harvest or even travelling into certain death. Starting an expedition just as winter is about to turn harsh could be lethal. Now many pagans, from many paths, not just those that actively embrace Celtic tradition, use this wheel of the year as a way to signpost and celebrate the key turning points of the year. The Celtic "quarter year" festivals are the points, the "sabbats" as many refer to them, that don't truly tie into any astronomical points of interest (because they tend to fall on the same dates each year), but roughly lay the year and the seasons into four sections, and try to mark the turning points in each.

One of these turning points is Imbolc, celebrated at the start of February, roughly half way between winter solstice and spring equinox: a celebration of the coming spring, making it through the harshest part of winter, and a time to honour Brigid, a goddess who, like the Morrigan, is often revered in triple form, and has many aspects. As mentioned previously, she is a patron to bards, and indeed I have found my own music more forth-coming after working with her at Imbolc, and have even written a song solely dedicated to her and the coming spring. She is a goddess of fertility and birth; hardly surprising as she is associated so closely with the return of spring, and the lambing season's start. She is the goddess of smithing and other crafts, and strongly linked with fire; it is no wonder at this cold, forbidding time of the year, when there is barely a warm breath to whisper of the spring to come, that such a person, such a goddess, would be drawn close to people's hearts. To cook, to craft, to make love and to keep fires burning - such human things are what bring hope and help us survive when the elements are against us.

Today, most of us have warmth and have shelter, and little to worry about in the way of food shortages. So what makes people like me turn to Brigid at Imbolc? The simple answer is we use the hunger and cold as a metaphor. Of course we don't want to be hungry, and we always make the wish that we never become literally hunger, and that we may honour the earth so that she may not hunger - through protection of resources and responsi-bility. However we also look to our spiritual selves to make sure that side of us is not being starved, and by this I don't mean simply on a theological or "other-worldly" plane, but simply how we behave in day to day life. Are we working so hard we run ourselves into the ground? Are we forgetting to take time out for our families? Have we lost touch with the things that make us who we are? Or are we happy, content in our life, working towards goals that are true, fit to ourselves, our purpose. Do we even know what that purpose is? Most people don't I guess, I'm pretty sure I change my mind every year!

This is a chance to celebrate if we have achieved over the winter what we set out to, be that as simple as weathering the winter with family, safe and warm, or perhaps a project or goal that we have been working towards. Sometimes it will be to remember oaths or goals that were set in place at previous festivals, often the previous Imbolc. Brigid is a point of focus to let us really look at the warm, caring, creative sides of ourselves, and remember that this doesn't just mean eating, having families and staying warm, but being a whole person, being kind, compassionate, and protecting ourselves when necessary - being strong, but not too hard. The strongest trees bend in the storm, they don't break, so we celebrate that we can weather what life throws at us and come back stronger, just like the sun returning after the long winter.

The next big celebration is Beltane, the lead-up to summer; May day, when the Hawthorn is in bloom and the sweet, pungent smell promises hot, sticky days to come. Fires are lit which have (or had) the dual purpose of encouraging the sun to continue his return, and also to lead livestock over to kill any ticks, lice or other parasites that may be plaguing them, especially in the warmer weather. My dad always taught me that people would often dance or leap over the fire too - and often this was as much about de-licing as it was about fun and festivity! We believe, and I have no idea if this is universal among people who follow Celtic traditions, that the veil is thin at this time, just as it is at Samhain, which is pretty close to the opposite side of the year if you look at it as a wheel.

What does this mean? Well, the veil is a widely used term

among Pagans which refers to the barrier between what we see, laughingly referred to as the real world, and that which is other-worldly; spirits, the dead, ghosts, gods, the fae, the sidhe. Is the veil a substantial wall which deteriorates at certain times of the year? I can't say, but I prefer to think of it like this: Everything exists all around us, all the time. We can't see it all the time, we'd go mad. So our brains, on a day to day basis, let us see and process pretty much what we need to get through our day. Those of us who are attuned, in some way, to pick up things on what I can only call a different "wave-length", may see more - some people all the time, others only when they try. For some reason, probably because of centuries of belief and people practicing certain rituals at these key points during the year, there are times when it is easier, when we can see, hear and feel things around us that we would normally struggle to perceive. This, for me, is what is meant by the thinning of the veil, although as a spiritual experience it is very much open to debate! So when the veil is thin, magic is easier, we are closer to our ancestors and give respect and honour to the deities/spirits that we feel close to. As well as being a fire festival and a solar celebration, Beltane is traditionally a time to purify oneself, protect oneself from negative influences and basically get rid of any baggage you've been carrying unnecessarily. It all goes on the fire and you look forward to the height of summer with a light and happy heart.

The other two big festivals are Samhain and Lughnasagh, and more festivals are celebrated including those that mark the astro-nomical points where days are longest, shortest or equal. So why is this so relevant in the twenty-first century? What does this structure mean to people who mostly deal with winter by putting the central heating on? How can celebrating the first harvest (Lammas, Lughnasagh) hold any meaning for someone who buys their grain at a supermarket and therefore has it available all year round? For me personally, I love to feel connected to the world around me in some way. So I will celebrate all eight of these turning points (any excuse for a good knees up!) as they each have their own unique significance. Each has an energy which if you pause and allow it, can flow through you, can be a part of you, and allow you to become a part of it, a part of the changing of the world, reminding us that nothing stays the same; we are always changing.

I am very conscious of the turning seasons. As described earlier, it's a wet day today. I see people all around me heads down, just wanting to get out of the rain, and I feel grateful for having the sense to *be* grateful, to appreciate that this cool shower will start the plants shooting up in the garden, will start the turn of the wheel towards warmer, longer days. So is this spirituality, or practicality? For me, a combination of both, a balance between appreciating what's there and where it's taking you, is key. Being closer to the earth, how it works, how things grow, helps us understand that we have a responsibility towards it; it's not ours, but we are a part of it, and because we take so much from it, we really have to give something back!

I think some people find conflict between following a pagan path and being part of modern society. Many of us lay claim to a harmony with nature and the earth, then drive miles and miles to get to some gathering or other, pumping out pollutants and pumping up that ever present carbon footprint! Yet I think it's important to remember that everything *is* about balance, using what you have, when you have to, and ensuring that any "bad" behaviour is offset in some way. Many people I know drive miles to get to Lime Tree Farm for various events, yet most of those people are also deeply involved in the conservation of the area, the promotion of living spaces for local wildlife and the prevention of the destruction of natural habitats for the creatures that already reside there. So there is no spurning of modern society and little hypocrisy, just a genuine desire to better understand the natural world, become a part of it rather than just living off it, and perhaps get a glimpse of life as it is without the trample of busy human feet.

There's so much to cover about how my Celtic heritage and my own study of Celtic legends and deities has intertwined with my life and created the person I am today, and I'm certainly not going to get through it all here. I'd like to think that those who are interested will go and look things up for themselves, and see if the Tuatha de Danaan can be relevant in their lives, or indeed look into your own heritage, and see if there is something there that you can make sense of in a modern world. For me, every season holds a new mystery, something to discover. Each cold spring morning pushes me towards something new. Each hot summer afternoon soaks my muscles in sensual stupor. Each crisp and golden autumn day is a treasure trove to explore with my son. And even when the winter bites hard and swift, my home is my hearth and centre, a safe haven where I live in the now and honour my ancestors, the path I came here on, and the Tuatha de Danaan who wind their way with story and song into a more magical tomorrow.

Listening to the Land I Walk on

Jane Meredith

When I was the resident Pagan in Lismore's Living Library people used to ask me what it meant to be a Pagan. The Living Library is an amazing community resource, where once a month volunteers gather together under different 'titles' representing their lives, such as *Living After Suicide*; *Refugee*; *Cancer Survivor*; *Community Activist* and *Pagan Priestess*. They are 'borrowed' by library users, who have up to a half-hour's conversation with their 'book'. Living Libraries began as a way of breaking down ignorance about others living in the same community, an ignorance that can result in bigotry, stereotypes and even violence. As a Living Book I explained again and again what it meant to be a Pagan.

Being a Pagan means I recognise that I am part of the earth. It means I follow the earth's seasons, and the turn of the moon and see myself and my life in terms of those cycles and seasons; that I relate to them personally. It means I believe we are all – all living things and the rocks and mountains and rivers as well – part of one complex, amazing planetary system. It means I pay attention to the birds that fly over my head, and the trees that grow around me and I have a living relationship with all these things. It means I listen to the land I walk on.

Lismore is a country town. It does have a university, but probably those people don't come to the town library much. Many of the people who borrowed the *Pagan Priestess* book that was me were farmers, or people who'd grown up on farms or in the country, or who had actively chosen to live in or retire to the country.

Again and again they looked at me in astonishment when they heard my definition of Paganism, and again and again they replied, "Well, I must be a Pagan, then". One woman told me how, as a child, the horses her parents kept talked to her. A man told me of walking on his land, how he tasted the earth to know when it was ready to be planted. Another man told me about sailing; how all it took was to be a few days out from land and you knew humans weren't in charge of anything, it was all wind and wave and a great force you could never fight but had to make love to, to survive. People told me of rivers they belonged to, of their relationship with dogs, of climbing trees as children and of knowing, always knowing that they were only a tiny part of life, but they felt the connections to everything else.

Some people, mainly women, told me they chose to call this connectedness God, though they knew it wasn't exactly what was talked about in church. Others told me that God meant nothing to them compared with the sunset over the land or the feeling they got when they stood outside and just breathed, or worked in their garden. I had some very interesting discussions, but the most amazing thing was how simple everything became. Once we knew we were talking about the same thing – this feeling of connectedness, of belonging, of being part of the earth and horses and rivers and sunset – there weren't any barriers. There was no theological argument to be had, we were discussing something so concrete, so obvious, so immediately and on-goingly present that all that was left was to tell each other stories of our lives.

Paganism is not abstract. It's not about things that might happen after we die, although a concern for and engagement with the long term well-being of the earth, beyond our individual lifespans, is a part of the sustainable thinking and activism many Pagans are involved in. It's not about what happened before we were born, either, although some of us have a fascination with the beginning of the universe, with ancient history or alternative social models. Pagan calendars are tied to seasonal events, whether that's the running of the salmon, the trees losing their leaves, wheat and barley ripening in the field, the whales passing up and down the coast or the bunya nut harvest. And because our calendars are tied to seasonal events, necessarily they are local. Bunyas grow in only a small part of Australia. The wheat ripens earlier in one part of Europe than another part. Only some rivers have salmon.

The Christian church celebrates Easter in springtime; except in the southern hemisphere, when it keeps to the calendar and so celebrates Easter in autumn. Its Christmas rituals are closely aligned with the winter solstice only a few days earlier; a divine child, the return of light and evergreen trees. Except in the southern hemisphere, when Christmas comes at the summer solstice and the church still celebrates the birth of a divine child, the return of light and evergreen trees. Paganism doesn't do that; we don't celebrate spring when it's autumn, or winter when it's summer. We open our eyes, look around us and see what's there. We breathe the air of the place we find ourselves in, we eat the food of that place and we know what season we're in. We attempt to walk lightly on the land, to respect it and operate in living relationship with it, caring for it as we do for our own bodies.

In Northern New South Wales every year I rediscover the wompoo pigeons; solid bright green birds with brilliant yellow bellies and purple throats, clustering in the fig in the corner of the garden. They only stay for a month or two, while the figs are ripe; chorusing their *wom-pooo* song to each other and swooping low across the lawn. The summer rains create a little stream; I can hear it from my bedroom, the sudden surprise of running water through a bed of lomandra and river lilies, planted because they can withstand and even revel in this occasional deluge. The river that I swim in rises or falls by several feet depending on rainfall; as I come down the path I often see the plop made by the invisible turtle, diving off its rock ledge to hide under water.

In Sydney the black cockatoos fly about singly and in threes and fours in autumn and winter, descending on a bottlebrush tree to devastate it, picking off every single flower and dashing it to the ground after they've eaten what they want, along with a branch or two if they feel like it. In late winter they start to flock together and suddenly I see twenty, thirty or more of them flying high across the suburb; a couple of times I've seen uncountable flocks, maybe several hundred birds flying together along the sea edge. In winter the light comes in my bedroom window at a particular angle in the early morning and throws red and gold light onto the wall where I have a picture hanging; it picks out patterns I've never seen before, so that I see greens where I've never seen green before, and the next day it lights the reds up like fire. The sea changes colour with the seasons. The sunsets have pink clouds in the east, in winter. I wait for the local asparagus to be in the shops, every spring.

As Pagans – and especially as Pagans who don't remain in the same place for generation after generation – we set ourselves up to learn from the land we live, work and create magic on. It is not just the landscape we are learning from, though certainly that will inform us; as we discover mountains or desert, jungle, coastal, forest or plains as our environment. The food that grows there; other plants that may be used for medicine, shelter or construction; and the animals, birds and insects that live there or journey though that environment will all inform us about the nature of that particular land. The weather, the length and severity of the seasons as well as the variations in these things from year to year will give us further information, further feeling for and understanding of this particular piece of earth.

We can also learn more by looking at, and seeking to under-stand the relationship earlier peoples had to this same place; people who did live in one place generation after generation, or people who travelled repeatedly or annually through particular landscapes. Their ways of relating to the land, when we are able to learn something of those, may grant us much more insight than simply a few years or one or two generations' worth of observations; especially if we don't initially have close ties to the land ourselves, through custom, inclination or lifestyle.

In Europe I was inspired again and again by the circles of standing stones, placed long ago by distant ancestors intent on marking special pieces of land as sacred, dedicating particular areas to ritual and ceremony. I was jealous. I wanted something like that on my own land, to practice my magic in. But how could I have a stone circle in Australia? It's true that some people create stone circles of their own; miniature ones in back gardens or larger ones in paddocks. There's a stone circle monument at Glen Innes made of forty granite monoliths, based on the Ring of Brodgar in the Orkneys, which is impressively huge. There are even standing stones in a roundabout, on the way to Byron Bay.

But creating stone circles is not what the indigenous people did, here. They didn't build things, or land-form, or cultivate, except sometimes using fire. They didn't make the river run over here instead of over there, or bring stones from hundreds of kilometers away or create hills and ditches where there weren't any. They didn't build dams, houses, halls, temples or villages. Instead, something quite special was done in this land we call Australia.

Here is a mountain. It is sacred. A river runs here sometimes, in the wet. It is sacred. There are caves in that cliff, they are sacred. These trees grow here and nowhere else; they are sacred. This is the waterhole. It is sacred. Here are the plains, the deserts, the forests, the sea. They are sacred. This is kangaroo, dolphin, kookaburra; they are sacred.

They looked at each thing, as it was, where it was, and saw it as sacred. They didn't need to move these things around or change their shape, form or use to find them sacred. They already were sacred. And it's easy to imagine that because they were sacred, they couldn't be interfered with. Digging up rocks from one place to take them somewhere else would be a violation of both places. Diverting a river would interrupt both the river's story and that of the land. The indigenous Australians' relationship to their land was one of sacredness at every step, seeing the landscape of their dreaming all around them; the sacred realm of becoming which is concurrent with ordinary time.

When I considered this – and I was on a bus in England as I was thinking about it – I realised it was showing me something important. People who've arrived in Australia over the last two hundred years have clumped things all over the place, especially around the edges of our landmass; shifting rocks and damming and chanelling rivers, plonking buildings and electricity plants and mines around as if it were a gameboard; as if to make up for the previous time that stretched back into infinity, where perhaps you couldn't tell the difference, in terms of landscape, from one stretch of ten thousand years to the next. But once we're out of the built landscape of cities we're reminded that sacred sites exist that have been sacred for far, far longer than we and our ancestors have trodden on this land.

That mountain's sacred to local Aboriginal tribes, they prefer that it isn't climbed. That tea tree lake is women's business, it used to be a birthing and ceremonial place. There's a bora ring out behind the old cemetery, they say it used to be an initiation place for young boys. Don't go inside the ring if you're a woman. These caves were sacred, people only go in them on special occasions.

And when I look at these places I see simply a mountain, a lake, a very slightly dented circle of land, a cave. But at the same time, I know they are sacred. And knowing that, I begin to look with different eyes. Eyes that inform me that if this lake, or this mountain is sacred, then why not every mountain and every lake? Most probably, every mountain and every lake. This one noted for the special colour of its rocks, that for its peculiar shape, another for its proximity to something else. Every piece of landscape, sacred already, simply for being what it is. And then reconfirmed as sacred, in our relating to it that way. All land is sacred land.

So I didn't build a stone circle.

Every Aboriginal person I've spoken to about this says we have to create our own relationship to the land. We can't have their relationship to it, as we weren't born to it; and we can't have no relationship, because this is where we live. So we must set out to create our own, living relationship with the land. This is what we have instead of stone circles.

I brought a piece of my heritage to this working, a model of the Wheel of the Year with its eight aspects. I took on one piece of observed learning from Aboriginal Australia; not to build anything but instead to enter into sacred relationship with what was there. And I let the two systems flow together. I began to look for eight points, on or around the perimeters of the Shire I lived in, that were sacred land. It is all sacred land, but I wanted definitive places, with public access, where we could go and do ritual, beginning to enter into our own sacred relating with this place.

I went into the east. I happened to live in Byron Shire, which has the eastern-most point of land of the Australian landmass. I went and sat there. I had been there many times before, but this time I went consciously as to sacred land with my eyes wide open and I observed its specialness. The air that rushes over those cliffs has come a long, long way across the sea, it's very fresh. Like air from the beginning of the world; sacred air. Standing out on the point there is sea stretching forever, in most directions. There were dolphins; there are often dolphins there.

I looked at the map. I looked west, far west. The Great Artesian Basin lay west of us, underground; a vast and secret water supply in this dry land. Informed by that, I looked closer west and found Rocky Creek Dam; man-made but twenty-five years old and by now landscaped with native trees and plants, beautiful in the setting sun, with ducks, black swans and other birds. Fresh water in this land of drought and scarcity; sacred water. It is peaceful, expansive and beautiful, a place of picnics and weddings and stillness.

I looked south, the direction of earth in the southern hemisphere Wheel. I went on many journeys south. I thought I was looking for rainforest, in this rainforest region but in the end what I found was a cave. A large cave, behind a waterfall; the water cascades into a round pool perfect for swimming. On full moon nights the moon rises across the pool; if you stand behind the waterfall it transforms into a shimmering curtain of silver, like the veil between this world and the other worlds, a portal.

Into each of the other directions I went, sometimes with others, sometimes alone. To the north-west lay a mountain, an extinct volcano. When we saw this on a map, although of course we already knew where it lay, the whole system came alive for us. Always and for many years our Circle casting had had an inexplicable bias.

We are in the southern hemisphere and we expect the north to be the height of our Circle; the direction of fire in a hot land, the sun's power, the summer solstice. But always, whoever was calling in the north-west overpowered, doubly and triply however the north had been called in. North caroled and the north-west boomed. North called for passion and warmth and the north-west shouted destruction and revelation. We never understood it until we looked at that map, looking for the power places, the distinctions in the landscape. A volcano. In the north-west. The volcano whose eruptions, more than twenty million years ago carved out this whole region, Byron Shire included; our whole Circle was birthed from this north-west point, and oriented towards it.

It seemed to tell us that our magic had, already, been operating with the land. That we had known these things we were just now discovering. That our Circle of Eight was just a way of understanding what was already there; just as the system of recognising the mountain or lake as sacred does not alter its sacredness, but our relationship to it. We never could find anything in the north to compete with that volcano. The point we settled on eventually was a small peak near the sea with fantastic views; almost all the rest of the Circle can be seen from there. And it has a fine view of the extinct volcano; and at the right time of the year you can watch the setting sun slide down its slope.

Searching the map again I looked for the centre of the Circle. Was it my own house, where we did many rituals and which lay in a valley surrounded by cliffs, valleys and trees? But right in the centre of the Shire, according to the map, was a privately owned tourist attraction; parklands with a shop and café. They had built a labyrinth there. A place for venturing into the centre, right at the centre. Even though it wasn't public land, we couldn't argue against it as the central point of this Wheel, this Circle of Eight. A labyrinth, let alone one surrounded by gum trees and other natives, was perfect.

All land in Australia can be called Aboriginal land, but some places more obviously than others. The eastern point of our Circle, Cape Byron, falls within the Cape Byron State Conservation Area, which is jointly managed by the Arakwal people and the State Government. I went to a talk there by a local Aboriginal ranger and she happened to mention there were different dreamings on different parts of this land. She said the Cape itself was Dolphin Dreaming, and a little further south, another beach which held our south-east point, was Sea-Eagle, or Sea-Hawk Dreaming.

After we'd established the eight points for our Circle I'd begun to look more closely at each of them, and especially I had a wish to recognise an animal for each of them. Dolphin had been my choice for the east, and sea-hawk for the south-east. This wasn't some miracle of convergence; all that had happened was the Aboriginal people had seen what was there – dolphins and sea-hawks – and we had gone to those same places and also seen what was there; dolphins and sea-hawks. It was not exactly surprising, but I heard it as a revelation. I felt it showed us we were on the right track; what we were doing was in genuine relationship to the land, and the land was talking with us.

I'm told the Aboriginal tribes indigenous to that area prefer that the extinct volcano is not climbed, and I don't climb it. There is a beautiful little walk around the base, which takes you immediately into deep forest and it's there I do my ritual, on the fertile slopes. There's another point, also, where our Circle of Eight intersects obviously with sacred Aboriginal land, and that's our south-west. In the southern hemisphere the south-west is the direction of mystery, the other realms; the direction – if you lay the Wheel of the Year over the compass – of Samhain.

I had a memory of an Aboriginal bora ring being somewhere out that way and we drove along back roads, searching, until we found it. What I hadn't remembered is that once off the road you have to drive through a small country cemetery to get to the bora ring. These two sacred sites sit side-by-side, sharing the same piece of land and both reaching into the spirit realms. I don't go inside the bora ring, but sit on the ground nearby. I listen to the magpies and watch the sun setting through the line of young gum trees. I try to imagine a time when there weren't paddocks all around, and a road nearby. I pour my offerings of water and honey onto the land and I make the ants happy. There are thousands of ants there; I think of them as the sacred animal for this direction, for after all they clean up the dead.

Listening to the land I walk on doesn't stop there. Sometimes I make time to go to one of these sacred places and spend half a day; listening, watching, feeling. I do small rituals of recognition, offering and thanks. I lie in the sun or discover the difference the seasons make, or the weather. My paths from place to place, and into the centre and back out again build up threads of connection, spiderwebs of energy and a magical overlay, at least in my own mind, that wasn't there before. In ritual, when I stand at any place within this large, spread out geographic circle and call to one of the directions I have immediate, layered and reverent connection with that place I'm calling to.

We've learnt so much about magic, and about the layers of this land through working with this Circle. When we call to the east, it's not an abstract concept we're calling to, but Cape Byron. If it is windy, or wet, or summer we feel how that will translate to that place, and therefore the energy of the east, on that day. When it's autumn we're situating ourselves, magically, at Rocky Creek Dam and sometimes we go there as well, to the direction of the season or Festival, to earth our ritual doubly into that place. For a special ceremony we choose our place; recently I went to the south-east with its fresh weather changes, the little beach you have to walk down a rocky path to, and performed a healing ritual. To me it's a place of hope and sunrises and sudden tidal changes and that's the energy I worked with and sent out.

This is local magic, earth magic, geographical magic. I didn't make it up out of my head, though my learning and thinking gave it a framework, an understanding and a formal structure. I found it by listening to the land; firstly my understanding of some of the ways Aboriginal relating to the land might inform me and next directly with the land itself; this mountain, this beach, this cave. I watched their stories of full moon, and of summer, and of wind and animal and plant. I brought them gifts of song, of offerings and listening. I opened my magic and ritual to them, and they spoke – as they had always been speaking – into the magic and into me.

Even away from that land I feel my connection to it, not in abstract terms but the exact observed and experienced cadences of early spring in the labyrinth, at the lookout, at the river mouth. We are still in conversation, even though I have gone away. Meanwhile I come to know another piece of land, a different magic but it is still the same magic, that Pagan essential of walking the land and listening to the land.

Parenting a Potentially Pagan Child

Nimue Brown

Plenty of people who come into paganism are parents, or go on to become parents. There are second generation pagans now going on to have children of their own, and there are plenty of pagans who hook up with people of a similar faith. As our community grows, our collective relationship with childhood becomes more relevant, because we have far more potentially pagan children now in the UK than we have had since Christianity caught on.

There is considerable diversity between groups and individuals when it comes to the issue of pagan children. Where moots gather in pubs, as they have tended to do for some time now, children can be unwelcome. This is as much about the nature of the venue and the timing as anything else. In the last decade, family friendly moots have become ever more prevalent, with coffee moots, walking moots and house moots allowing younger people to attend. Some aspects of pagan practice lend themselves more to family participation than others. Where serious magical work is undertaken, ritual nudity is a feature, or deep trance work is sought, the setting may be deemed inappropriate for those under eighteen. However, not all adults wish to work in these ways, and so the child friendly options are opening up. We have increasing numbers of people who like pagan rites of passage and the odd seasonal celebration, but who have no desire to strip off or to invoke anything. Twenty years ago, paganism was far more inherently adult. Whether the presence of children in that generation changed this, or the change that let more children in came from adult participants who wanted something less intense, I have no idea.

The first question a pagan parent must consider is whether a child can be, or should be, a pagan. Twenty years ago most pagan groups I knew of were wary, at best, of anyone under eighteen. Historical associations between paganism and Satanism have made many pagans in the past afraid that they would be accused of Satanic ritual abuse. Fear of Social Services meant that my generation were not all that included as children. Times have changed, Social Services are a lot more open minded, and on the whole we have fewer reasons to be fearful. But that alone is not enough reason to bring children up as pagans, when you consider the counter-arguments.

As we have no formal doctrine, it's widely held that to be a pagan must be not only a deliberate, personal choice, but a conscious and ongoing act of engagement. We don't baptise, we don't issue a few stock phrases, and we don't go round converting people. Are our own children able to choose a pagan path? It is as morally objectionable to force paganism on them as it would be to inflict it on anyone else. But at the same time, the desire to share values, and the practical advantage of being able to take the kids to gatherings, means they are being exposed to a religion.

Deliberately excluding your offspring from your religion feels very peculiar, at best. Come their teens, any attempts to tell them that magic is off limits, will push them towards it. Enough of us were paganly-minded teenagers to know that process all too well from the other side. Childhood literature is full of wizards and fairies, so kids tend to be attracted to pagan magic, but are not equipped to understand it. Spiritual and magical paths call for self discipline, self awareness and a degree of understanding no one can ask of a child. And yet, every child wants access to the world of the adults around them.

Finding ways of talking about what we do, without indoctrinating a young mind, is challenging indeed. Involving children in celebrations, rites of passage in their own lives, and the broadly green spirituality of paganism can be enriching, but it is not easy.

Especially not if you want to make sure of raising a child who can think independently and who is not just swallowing your own beliefs. So many of us came to paganism because we were escaping the religions forced on us by our own families. Replicating that serves no one. Ultimately it may push the next generations away, but we run the same risk if we do too much to exclude them. As is often the case with pagan life, there are some very fine balances to achieve here.

Normal life exposes children to a great deal of fantasy. There's the tooth fairy and Father Christmas for a start. Some parents (irrespective of faith) go to great lengths to raise children in a safe little reality bubble of their own, where no bad things happen, dead pets are magically replaced, dead relatives are just having a sleep, and so forth. We have a culture of lying to children, and we do this, in theory, to protect them. Of course it means that the process of finding out the truth about life is that bit more traumatic, laced with the bitter knowledge of having been lied to. Growing up normal can mean horrible disillusionment. All aspects of paganism are about life as it really is – from the honouring of death and the dead, to a healthy recognition of sex, and all places in between. We have our own stories, and many traditions do include ideas about magic. How do we say to children, 'We lied to you about that fantasy thing, but this one is real?' Negotiating a child through the standard pretences of childhood is more difficult if honour demands that you tell the truth. Finding age-appropriate language and explanations that make sense without misleading, is not easy. However, doing this is a good investment if you hope to be able to talk to a slightly older child or a teen about deity, trance work, spells and shape shifting.

I think in many ways it pays to bring up children to be sceptical. Asking questions is healthy, and doubt is one of the greatest protections against fraud and other forms of psychological abuse. Children who know how to question are less vulnerable to self-interested gurus, or the predators who lurk along every spiritual path. Children who know how to trust their own perceptions, and who are not forever being told that everything depends on forces, and reasons beyond their knowledge, will make better choices. And if in time, they do choose to become pagans, that ability to doubt will not have hurt them. Religious experience is about direct, individual moments of awe and wonder. An open, questioning mind is, if anything, more equipped to recognise the numinous than one that has been nailed shut out of fear.

My experience of pagan parents is that, by mainstream standards, we are entirely 'alternative'. In a culture where it is normal (I have been told) to just order one's offspring about, pagans are more likely to treat their own children with respect. New developments in education favour child-led learning, so there are plenty of rational arguments out there to back up the idea of child-centric parenting. Anecdotal evidence inclines me to think that pagan parents are more active than average in their parenting. We listen to our children, encourage them to have their own views, feelings and ideas. This is a natural consequence of not wanting to be dogmatic with them. Paganism tends towards an absence of hierarchy, and this too can reflect in our parent-child relationships, where we may be less interested in who has authority, and more interested in who has the best ideas. For a natural anarchist, a parent who finds the arbitrary use of power an affront, and does not believe in blind obedience to God the Father, King and Country, or anything else that smacks of tyranny, regular parenting is out. Traditional parenting and traditional parental authority belongs to a patriarchal system that anyone who has ever honoured a goddess finds it hard to uphold.

Many pagans are animist, seeing spirit as present in all things. This of course includes our own children. We aren't encountering blank slates, unformed adults, or small irritations, but spirit-laden manifestations of nature. They are the inevitable consequence of fertility worship! Children are part of the nature we honour, and that makes it easier for us to respect them. Pagan parents talk about the way their children quest and question, enthralled by how their offspring understand the world. We learn from them just as they learn from us. It creates a very different power balance from your 'standard' parent-child dynamic where total control lies on one side and only pester power on the other. A more balanced, pagan dynamic can shock people who are on the outside of it, and who have rigid beliefs about the nature of childhood, children, and parenting. There are still plenty of people (some of them in positions of power and authority) who see children as innocent, blank slates, to be kept away from all 'adult' issues. Often the same people will take no issue with a diet of television, fast food, and the raising of children who cannot make risk assessments for themselves and who have never poked a stick into mud.

There is increasing evidence that children need nature in their lives, and that conventional parenting often deprives them of this. The Forest Schools movement has long since established that children learn more and develop better socially and emotionally, for spending time out of doors. Ideally with trees. It suggests that being a pagan child is going to be good for you. Whatever else a nature based religion does, or does not do for a child, it takes them outside, every chance it gets. Enabling children to go out is vitally important. As it becomes more culturally normal to keep our children shut away like we do our factory reared animals, children might be going to need significant support to grow up free range and emotionally healthy. If the computer games, television and internet are supposed to be the focus of life, the child who is not chained to a device is going to be in a strange place, socially. But the free range child is also in a position to enable other children to break from captivity.

The easiest way to introduce children to paganism is simply by engaging them with the natural cycles. Time spent with the sun and rain, poking about in mud, feeding ducks, and so forth will teach them about nature. Anything on top of that is a bonus. It is easy to craft family celebrations at key points in the year – they need not be big or complicated. Many pagan parents that I've met tend to avoid including deity in family ritual. Helping children form a sense of the land, its inhabitants, and their ancestors gives you plenty to work with. A broad sense of 'spirit' is easily included. As children grow, they ask questions about what it's for, and what it means. Giving them the space to find their own answers is important. Again, so many of us came to paganism to avoid dogma, there is no incentive to dish it out to our children. What they come to understand for themselves is going to be far more powerful and enduring than anything we try to tell them. What they feel, will stay with them, whoever they decide to be in later life.

Children in group rituals present all kinds of interesting challenges. It is in the nature of children to be restless, have shorter attention spans and a willingness to make noise. They also cannot be relied upon to pick up cues for silence, stillness or any other kind of cooperation. If a ritual calls for deep working it can be tempting to control the disturbances as much as possible. Also, deep working is likely to be dull for younger participants. Where ritual is primarily for celebration and families are antici-pated, crafting livelier rituals is not difficult. In theory, everyone can work at their own level, but in practice this kind of public gathering is more party-like and less conducive to soul searching. However, meaningful experience is not just about soul searching, and those bonds of community are important, so child friendly rituals should never be discounted as an option.

I wonder about how our ancient ancestors handled the inclusion of children. Of course, for the Celts there would have been only their own culture and faith (at least until the Romans showed up). The idea of not bringing your children up precisely to follow your own religion is, as far as I know, a new one. I have the impression that religion was far more intrinsic for our Celtic ancestors. It wasn't something to do at the weekend. There was no distinction between belief and life. When all of the life experience a child has reflects the faith position of the tribe, the ideas I've suggested about delineation and separation become a nonsense. Most of our children do not grow up in a pagan context. There are likely to be non-pagan grandparents, peers, teachers, and the vast array of media at their disposal. Our children are exposed to a great many beliefs, values and attitudes, such that they (or for that matter, we) cannot hope to have a smooth relationship between belief and life. Modern paganism requires interactions with a diverse, complex and occasionally unfriendly world. Even though we can teach our children that values and morality apply to all aspects of life, all life is not pagan, because of the small detail of everyone else.

Schools in the UK are becoming increasingly pagan-friendly. This is in no small part due to having to accommodate children from all manner of other faith backgrounds. Teachers can no longer assume that their classes are Protestant Christian. A child may be the only pagan in the school, but they won't be the odd one out. Even in small, rural schools, there may be a lone Jehovah's Witness, a couple of Muslims, a few atheists … So long as there isn't a total hegemony of faith, being a lone pagan child is no great issue. However, the vast majority of teachers and head teachers have no idea what 'pagan' really means, much less how any given path within it functions. No matter how well meaning they are, they will not know what to do with your pagan child, unless you take the time to tell them.

My personal experience of this to date has been wholly positive; I have only ever encountered interest and support. Not all pagan parents have as easy a time of it though. A lot depends on how much special dispensation you want for your child as a consequence of your faith. Eight festivals off in a year may cause you problems, where one can more likely be accommodated.

Asking for variations on the same perks children of other faiths get, is often fine, but push beyond that and you can encounter hostility. This has nothing to do with faith, and everything to do with being perceived as taking the piss! The same is true when dealing with hospitals, social workers or any other manifestation of power. We are entitled to the same rights and fair treatment as everyone else. Normally, we should expect to get it. If we stray into the realms of the ridiculous, we should not expect to be pandered to.

Bullying is far less tolerated in schools than it used to be. The culture of diversity and multiculturalism benefits pagan children a great deal. All sorts of eccentricities can and will be tolerated in more liberal schools. However, there are also schools where high levels of conformity to social norms are still expected. From the outside, it's not always easy to judge the culture. It pays, therefore, to send pagan children out into the world equipped to cope with it. However much we might want to raise them in a safely pagan cocoon, they need to be able to survive. We might stall that process with home schooling, but even so the day will come when they need to fly the nest. However old they are, they need to be equipped to survive in environments that will not necessarily suit them. The desire to protect and nurture is intrinsic to good parenting, and pagan parents are much like everyone else in this regard. Again there is a balance to strike here.

Modern pagan parenting is very much at odds with the mainstream. While the science increasingly suggests we're going the right way, there are a great many reactionaries out there who feel threatened by raising children as people, and by the idea of the free range child. It's easy to raise a child by tethering them to a few bits of technology and leaving them to it. However, the consequence is not a happy, healthy or independent creature. Children need nature. They need to be respected and listened to. The current culture that bombards them with sexual imagery but is horrified by the sexuality inherent in some forms of paganism is a sick culture. How we raise our children is likely to become an ever more important political issue. As more children are raised by nursery schools, after-school clubs and childminders, the relationship between state and parent gets ever more complex. As the evidence stacks up for more natural parenting and less pressured childhoods, we may be ahead of the game, but it's unlikely to make us popular.

It may seem that pagan parenting is only an issue for those pagans who get into breeding. It isn't. The politics of childhood shapes the future for all of us. The controls we place on parenting or the freedoms we demand for it have wide reaching social implications. Whether or not we have children of our own, anyone who isn't solitary may at some point need to tackle the issue of children at moots and rituals. Sometimes it's easier when those children turn up with a pagan parent, but sometimes they don't. What we do with young people who may not be eighteen yet, and may not have parental support, and who want to be pagan and to learn, has always been a minefield. I don't anticipate that becoming less of an issue any time soon. What happens when someone else's young child announces a desire to be pagan?

When our own children have strange, magical, or spiritual experiences, we handle them. We sit those uncanny moments of knowing, the portentous dreams, past life memories, fairy sightings and everything else into a context that makes it ok to talk. Pagan parenting will involve as much unpicking of fantasy from reality as any other kind, but if our child thinks they've seen a ghost, we won't disregard them. We also won't troupe them off to the doctor and demand psychological assessment if they have an imaginary friend, or we catch them playing with a dead twin they didn't know about and we can't see. But what happens when someone else's child is going through all these same, very pagan experiences? I know a number of adults with poor mental health whose stories make me suspect that a pagan upbringing would have left them much happier and more functional. We would not want the state to interfere in our own parenting, or for anyone to tell us that we can't support little Taliesin when he thinks he's talking to his dead granny. The other side of that is that we are in no position to think the government should tell our neighbours not to be so hard on little Jonny when he's talking to his dead grandmother.

One of the things that pagan children tend to learn early on is that the world is not a very easy place to live in. But if we raise them to be creative, passionate people who know how to love and respect the world, then they will help to shape a different sort of future. Maybe they will be pagans. They may choose to be Klingons instead, or atheists, or go forth to invent a whole new way of looking at the world which leaves us dazed and confused. All we can do is give them the best understanding we have, and trust them.

The Way of the Web: A Case Study in Online Pagan Experience

James Middleditch

Paganism and the internet may not seem to be the most immediate of bedfellows. The first, prioritising direct experience of the real, natural world could be seen to be the antithesis of the second, which provides only mediated experience, dependent upon and filtered through manufactured technology. I want to challenge this view, and outline ways in which the practice of Paganism can be celebrated and enhanced through the technology of the internet. Some may find these ideas to be a mutation of the natural purity of Pagan ideals; others may accept this as a contemporary evolution of an ancient way of life, providing new and unique opportunities that stay true to its spirit and intention.

My focus is on social networking, and is drawn from the experience of having helped to set up and administer an online group called The Mystik Way, which has a significant Pagan leaning. Established in February 2011, the Facebook group gained 900 members in its first year, with approximately 4,000 having signed up to regular updates by the end of its second. Two significant forces behind the group are both in their 60s, having lived the experience of Paganism, among other paths, for decades. The experiences described here, therefore, while rooted in the present, emerge from patterns witnessed across the second half of the twentieth century, to the unique moment in spiritual development that is here, the start of the second decade of the new millennium. My aim is not to provide a theoretical framework for this development; others have done this by mapping the cybercultures of neopaganism and technopaganism in more objective ways. My aim is to provide a summary of real

Pagan experience as enlivened by the new technologies of social networking.

Tracing this development will reveal a significant movement from the individual to the collective. The most common representation of Pagan practice in the twentieth century focused on either solitary or small group experiences. Accepted as an alternative, rather than mainstream life choice, Paganism could be a lonely experience. This is not necessarily a bad thing, and many aspects of Paganism emphasise the importance of solitary experience, particularly within the natural world, developing from Romantic experiences of the sublime in epic natural landscapes in the eighteenth and nineteenth centuries. Local groups, focalising around nearby natural landmarks and locations, have risen, fallen and risen again across the decades. Defined often by geography and landscape, time and culture have also played a part in these groups; promises of the 1960s seemed to be deferred until the pre-millennial excitement of the 1990s. But the evolution of Paganism I wish to describe does not emerge with the spread of the internet into people's homes at the dawn of the twenty-first century. Having felt the potential for a spiritual resurgence in Paganism at the turn of the millennium, myself and the members of my Pagan-orientated meditation group would instead feel a disappointing dissipation during the first decade of this 'new era'. Our direct experience of nature, our observing of the Wheel of the Year and our dedication and learning would continue, but our numbers appeared to be dwindling rather than growing.

As with many cybercultures the explosion came with the arrival of social networking, and the increased access to online communities, first through broadband and then through smart-phone and wireless technology. This new way of interacting with the internet is often referred to as Web 2.0, its distinguishing feature being the ability of users to produce and publish material instead of simply consuming that produced by those with the technological power to do so. Perhaps it is the innate freedom and democracy of this new possibility that marries so well with Pagan beliefs, which emphasise individual truth rather than collective doctrine. Solitary and small group experiences could now be recorded and transmitted in a less mediated fashion, rather than being dependent on a small number of media producers, who would either ignore Paganism as being too alternative or worse, use the distorting mirror of representation and stereotype in the examples seen in film and television over the decades.

The result is a proliferation of online Pagan networks such as The Mystik Way. These groups unify smaller groups and many solitary practitioners, providing the first truly worldwide sharing of Pagan experience. Of course, we should not fall into the obvious trap of ignoring those cultures which are currently excluded from cyberspace either through lack of resources or through more rigorous censorship. However, it should be celebrated that we have never before been able to so easily share experiences across so many different continents and countries, so that a solitary Pagan practice can be witnessed, commented upon, even joined in, by geographically diverse people, within moments. To take a romantic view, the spiritual sharing of experience has, through the medium of technology, surpassed the physical boundaries that had once separated it.

This postmodern collapse of spatial distances lends itself beautifully to Paganism and the appreciation of nature. Photography is one of the key features of the modern, shared Paganism witnessed in The Mystik Way and other online groups. This aspect takes a number of forms, a primary example of which is the sharing of areas of special Pagan significance such as ley line hubs like Glastonbury Tor and Stonehenge. These iconic images, familiar to many Pagans across the world, can now be part of their daily experience. Significant dates, particularly solstices, can be shared by a whole online group, even if only one member attends. While a cynic may lament the replacement of live experience with a mediated one, and claim that a photograph cannot compete with the 'real thing', I would take a more imaginative view, which places more creative power in the group's members. Places, of course, have energy; this may be foreknown ley line energy, or an energy unique to a time of year, weather pattern or lighting, drawing a distinctive and tangible power from the location. Pagan experience includes the visual stimulation of such places as the first step to a deeper, extra-sensual appreciation of these energies. Shared photographs can prompt these moments, as well as widening the experience to include sights that because of practical barriers, one may never set their eyes upon in the physical world.

Commonly shared images on The Mystik Way include locations in New Zealand, where key members live and practice not just appreciation of natural beauty above land, but underwater too. Through the medium of the online group, those of us on the other side of the world can tune in to these distinctive and faraway energies, and feel them as if we were there. Anecdotally, one of the most heart warming and supportive roles played by such photographs is to those who have physical impairments that now prevent them from experiencing the outdoors as fully as they might like. Areas of wilderness and isolation, found through adventure and physical effort, are available to all, no matter their health. The visual stimulation of photography can transmit the energies, and provoke both wakeful and deep meditations, in which the two-dimensional image on the computer screen becomes an immersive inner space within the mind's eye. The advantage to the photographer is also new and unique; if solitary experience was desired, this can be maintained, and yet the shared experience of discussion and mutual appreciation can then be initiated and enjoyed by posting the photo to the group. On a wider scale, this idea also fascinatingly adjusts the traditional way of experiencing the Wheel of the Year, as opposing

Sabbats are celebrated simultaneously across different hemispheres, reminding us all of the constant turning of the Wheel, and sharing the energies of different points and seasons across these great distances.

Photographs do not have to be of natural, outdoor spaces to contribute to the online Pagan experience. Smaller scale, domestic settings can lead to even more powerful sharings of energies. Many people like to share images of their altars, adorned by totems and objects of special significance to them. This has been said to empower the altar, particularly for solitary practitioners who may have had to keep such places private or even secret. The appreciation of the personal sacred space provides it with energy, just as all appreciation can send positive energy to a focalised point. These small spaces can also act as conduits to much bigger exchanges of energies.

One of the most popular and successful aspects of The Mystik Way, which embraces the Pagan tradition of healing with energy, is called the Healing Link. It is held at 9pm GMT every evening, and requires participants to momentarily 'link in' to the group. Some people use the focal point of the altar of the founder of the group, which is sent with the reminder of the impending moment each day. Others simply take a moment to close their eyes and acknowledge the process, accepting that it is happening on an intangible, spiritual level and therefore not needing the visual stimulus. The altar contains traditional Pagan iconography, to appeal to common, archetypal roots in the act of sharing and sending energy with intent to heal, and to tap into the common psychic responses triggered by such objects as a pentagram, a candle flame, and a chalice. Having used the image of the altar to collect the energy, the group trusts that it is distributed appropriately. A list is used to facilitate this, upon which people are added who members feel would benefit from some of this healing energy. Nature itself is often the recipient of the collected energy; we are frequently reminded to send our thoughts to animals and pets, as well as trees, plants and natural landscapes, particularly those that may be under threat. While of course there are many traditional parallels in other spiritual and religious practices including prayer itself, it is another aspect to be celebrated that an individual can name someone that several thousand people then see, and for a moment, send their best wishes to, without ever having personally met.

As this practice becomes increasingly popular it also becomes exponential; different and distinctive groups now join together at set times and dates, to share in bigger and bigger energy exchanges. The effects of this cannot be guessed at, as the focalising of so much energy around the principles of nature, healing and unconditional love has never been possible with such ease. One uncanny aspect of the practice is the common, instinctive belief in its ability to work. Many people describe this practice as having come easily to them, as if it is something fundamental to our potential as human beings, which we have always had the potential to do, but are only now able to realise on such a grand scale.

Community thus becomes a key word associated with this type of practice. Various views are held about the relative values of 'online communities', but considering the aforementioned often solitary nature of Paganism, as well as the huge geographical diversity of members, it undoubtedly holds great benefits. One of the most significant of these is the exchange of information, either to educate or to expand knowledge about Paganism and associated pathways. The founders of The Mystik Way have been very careful not to attach any particular label to the content, discussions or belief systems of the members, instead using the more inclusive word 'spiritual' in the group's official description. This has resulted in a fascinating range of Pagan 'strands' having emerged within the group, alongside explorations of aspects of many other religions and belief systems that members wish to discuss or explore. It quickly became clear how varied, and yet how unified Paganism is around the world; despite differences, there is a common core that only becomes apparent with so many varied voices contributing to a single group. For younger Pagans or people who have discovered this pathway later in life, this multitude provides a fascinating range of options from which to pick a preferred practice, but equally, the learning never ends for more established members.

The strands that intertwine within the group are many and varied. Avalonian imagery, focusing on both mythical and contemporary experiences of Glastonbury play an important part, perhaps because this Somerset town is a crucial inspiration to such open spiritual groups as The Mystik Way. This leads seamlessly into the Goddess worship and Earth mysteries strands, which in turn sit well with a strong ecological awareness. Drawing inspiration from beyond the Earth itself, astrology makes a regular appearance, as do other divining methods such as tarot cards. These strands find unity in a strong Kabalistic element, with explorations of the Tree of Life and regular accounts of ritual and elemental magic. In turn these prompt discussions of other magical and energy based systems such as crystal healing and chakras, sound healing and meditation. The prevalence of such practices in Glastonbury brings us full circle, in a way that truly characterises the paradoxically varied yet unified approach to contemporary Paganism.

A community made up of such varied influences leads naturally to creativity, which is one of the other central pillars of this type of spiritual practice. As well as photographs of real places, members also embrace opportunities to create their own interpretations or explorations of various Pagan pathways. Painting and artwork are prevalent, lending a more imaginative and meditative ingredient to the visual stimulus of the previously mentioned photographs. These include members' own tarot cards and representations of Kabalistic diagrams. Poetry is a major strand of this type of creativity, finding a natural home in a place whose practices includes the ritual readings, affirmations and chants. Both of these elements come from rich traditions, and the discussion opportunities of such an online group allows the creative process itself to be explored, illuminating not only inspirations from real life artists and poets, but the spiritual benefits of a creative mind.

The twin pillars of knowledge and creativity very quickly manifested in a magazine for The Mystik Way group, which has been produced online once a month since April 2011. Each issue is made up of the strands discussed previously, and many more. It again embodies the principles of community and contribution; many people who would not have known where to have shared their thoughts, knowledge and creations have found a home for them in the magazine. It acts as both a permanent and evolving record of contemporary Pagan experience. Taking us back to our original claim, it is also something that can only exist here and now. It is edited and created primarily by two people, one who lives in the United Kingdom, the other in New Zealand. Only the internet can provide the real-time links and speed of transfer that enables such a collaboration; editorial discussions and decisions over content, design and layout occur by email and webcam. The articles themselves are gathered electronically from all across the world. The distribution and consumption of the magazine both follow this production model; it is read online, downloaded, printed perhaps, wherever in the world the reader happens to be, as long as internet access is there. It can be tempting to become too familiar with this type of practice, now that it forms such a considerable part of people's daily lives, both personally and professionally, and forget how extraordinary it is. But as a modern way of developing a Pagan community based on real, shared experience, it is remarkable. For a practice that prides itself on its ancient roots, the fusion of modernity and antiquity is inspiring, and surely gives hope for a rich future.

Tracking changes across time, from past through present and into future, is one final aspect worth exploring. One of the common words that binds various strands of Pagan and other spiritual thought is 'energy'. This can be an individual's personal energy, the collective energy of groups, or the energy of places and the Earth itself. These aspects have been discussed already, but one of the fascinating elements of The Mystik Way is its ability to map changes, as energies rise, fall and evolve over months, weeks, even individual days. We all respond to energy shifts, whether consciously or unconsciously. By sharing our instinctive response to energy levels, we can discover crucial patterns that may have been hidden in the past. We can discover whether the energy shifts are unique to ourselves, and thus work out a plan to change or work with these energies. More fascinating though is when discussion reveals a commonality of energy levels, even across different continents. The early days of The Mystik Way coincided with what is now known as the Arab Spring, and various discussions explored the energetic changes that surrounded this, as well as possible spiritual readings of it such as that prophetically described in James Redfield's *The Twelfth Insight*, which had been published at the same time. Much discussed dates have been and gone, such as the December 21st 2012 Mayan calendar climax, and energy patterns have been shared and comparisons made.

It is through such discussions that much important observations are discovered. In the latter half of the previous decade, various coincidences and texts seemed to herald a rise in feminine energy on a wide scale, and balance between the two complementary forces of masculine and feminine seemed to be of paramount importance. This has formed much of the discussion on The Mystik Way, with a surprising amount of people having noted the same subtle, intangible shift over the past few years, but perhaps never having been given a chance to 'triangulate' it with others, and confirm the trend. It is noticeable in the very language and imagery of the group, as we have come to discover that there is a commonality, worldwide, which seems to come instinctively. Various greetings, blessings and references to energies and connections come easily there, even if they are rarely spoken aloud in members' everyday lives. The emotional imperative of balanced, unconditional love, another common principle in Pagan groups and practice, is woven throughout the exchanges that occur throughout each day.

All of these things provide a foundation which assumes that certain qualities override old, divisive thinking, and embrace a new, more balanced future, in which we as human beings increasingly reflect the natural balance of the planet itself. Biological gender becomes secondary to the goal of achieving harmony between our masculine and feminine sides. Nationality becomes secondary to our common humanity, and old boundaries and divisions between cultures are overridden by a shared desire to explore. Age, health and ability become secondary to our potential to contribute to a community based on kind words and inspirational imagery. Religious or spiritual belief itself becomes secondary to a shared desire to talk, and discover, and grow; labels, even the label 'Pagan', while held in respect, reduce in significance. We become inhabitants of the Earth, rather than our separate units of habitation, whether they be home, city, state or country. We also become aware of our non-human neighbours, from animals and pets to plants and trees. Our relationship to them, and our need to take care of them, becomes heightened.

Of course it is beyond our capacity to determine whether this foundation is going to hold, across the many social and technological changes that are no doubt ahead of us. However, trends that have been gathered through research such as the 2011 United Kingdom census show us that the change may already be gathering pace, with the number of people identifying themselves exclusively as Christianity having fallen by approximately four million in ten years, while those identifying themselves as having 'no religion' has risen by 10 per cent in the same time. Paganism is now the second highest 'other religion', with over 56,000 people identifying themselves as such, and more having separately identified as Wiccan, spiritual and pantheistic. The religious and spiritual landscape is changing, in line with predictions held by many Pagan and other spiritual writers over the last few decades. How this continues to change over the next decade and beyond will be fascinating to discover, and the contemporary experience of online communities will be a useful gauge and record.

To return to our starting point, and acknowledge once more the fears of some, that increasing dependence on the internet will lead to fragmentation and reliance on mediated, rather than real, experience, I hope that this summary of live online Pagan communities will have allayed some of these concerns. Pagans and other spiritual practitioners have always used tools, often distinguishing themselves from organised religion by using tools that are easily found or made, available to all rather than the privileged. The laptop, mobile phone, wireless connection and social networks are just the latest tools to be employed in the ancient urge to increase our connection to our fellow humans and animals, plants and trees, mountains and streams, earth and sky. We have collectively, perhaps unconsciously, gathered resources and manifested them into these forms, which now act as portals to an intangible world of shared experiences, ideals and hopes. And while intangible, groups such as these are enhancing the experience of Pagans and others seeking a spiritual dimension to their lives in real and measurable ways. As such, for however long they continue, and for the lasting changes they will undoubtedly bring in ways both big and small, they should be celebrated.

A Week in Pagan London

Lucya Starza

Opening the Veil

Thursday, 31 January, 2013

I am in the heart of London and a ritual is about to begin; a ritual to celebrate Imbolc, the start of spring.

I am a witch – a Gardnerian Wiccan to give a precise name to my tradition – but the ritual I'm waiting to take part in is no Wiccan rite. This is Enochian magic – sixteenth-century magician John Dee's Opening of the Veil. According to the description by those running it, the Pagan Federation London and the Path of Fire, 'The ritual will draw on both English Elizabethan and Chinese classical mystical traditions.' How eclectic.

But then, this is pagan London; a melting pot – or a cauldron – of magical ideas. It always has been. I predict it always will be. Right now, I believe pagan London is in the springtime of a Golden Age.

London's origins are themselves the material of pagan legend. According to Geoffrey of Monmouth, in *The History of the Kings of Britain*, the city was founded by the Trojan Brutus as England's ancient capital.

This is myth, of course, not academic history, but a relic some attribute to Brutus still stands. The London Stone – a worn limestone block caged in the wall of a bank in Cannon Street – has been said to be the altar stone Brutus set at the heart of the temple he built when he founded this great city.

A more realistic explanation is that the London Stone is an ancient milestone, but I would argue that London is not just a city built of stone and brick and mortar. It is also a city built of myths and legends. It is a city that stands on both sides of the veil. There is a London in the material world and in the realm of the spirits, gods, angels and ancestors; in the realm of stories, of imagination – the wellspring of magic.

And here I am, about to open that veil using the magic of John Dee, with a large group of pagans from all traditions – and a little bit of Chinese mysticism to boot (Imbolc is also the time of Chinese New Year after all, and London does include its own wonderful Chinatown).

It is hard to be a pagan Londoner without being eclectic. It isn't impossible. There are solitary practitioners who keep themselves to themselves, following one tradition or another and believing that the Old Ways should not be tampered with. But I don't think that's the London current. If you are a pagan who likes to get out and socialise, then you are likely to end up more fusion than tradition.

Tonight's ritual is taking place at London's Conway Hall, which describes itself as, 'The landmark of London's independent intellectual, political and cultural life.' It was opened in 1929 and is run by the Ethical Society to promote free thought, particularly on religion. Above the main stage are the words, 'To thine own self be true.' I've seen them at countless pagan conferences and rituals over the years. They echo the Wiccan Rede: 'An it harm none, do what ye will.' Yet they are words that humanists who meet at Conway Hall can also abide by.

This open ritual is in one of the side halls; an oblong room with windowless walls but a glazed ceiling through which we can see the starry night sky above, even allowing for London's light pollution. It feels as though we are entering a temple. Robed ritualists purify us with droplets of salt water and incense smoke as we pass through the doorway.

The room is lit only by candles – we are given one each to hold. We are asked to form an inner and an outer circle, then to move deosil, or sunwise, in a slow walking meditation. Words are added – they are Enochian words, repeated as a mantra. The magic builds through song, chant and incantation; the opening of the veil.

It is Imbolc, the time for new beginnings. This is magic to plant seeds of hopes and dreams within each of us, so that they may grow to fruitfulness in the year to come. We are asked to place our candles on the altar in the centre of the room, and then to take a few real seeds – sunflower seeds – from a bowl there. We open the circle, the rite is ended and it is time for food and drink and socialising. All around I hear people saying what a lovely ritual it was, a beautiful eclectic blend of Eastern and Western mysticism, of the old and the new.

The seeds of the future have been planted in the fertile soil of the past. This to me is what contemporary paganism is all about.

Imbolc at the Covenstead
Friday, 1 February, 2013
It is Imbolc, and I am with my coven. As I said before I am a Gardnerian Wiccan, but I haven't always been.

Every modern witch has a witchy granny, don't they? Except my granny wasn't a witch – or a Wiccan – she was a Theosophist and worked as an astrologer. She didn't much approve of Wicca. 'Too much nudity,' she once told me.

Nevertheless, it was my grandma who taught me the Wiccan Rede – although she didn't call it that. To her it was just good, sensible advice. 'You can do whatever you want, so long as you don't hurt anyone by doing it,' she explained. It was advice I took to heart. Only after becoming a Wiccan did I realise where the idea came from.

I came to Wicca in the mid 1990s. I was at another Pagan Federation London open ritual. I think it might even have been another Imbolc. In the social after the ritual I was invited to a training evening run by a Wiccan coven.

I went along to see what it was like and came back to every training evening for a little over a year before being initiated. The people I am with tonight were all initiated in that same coven. The ritual we are to perform has been done many times before. It has been handed down from sister coven to sister coven so often it has become part of our heritage and tradition.

The ritual is about to start; the words are secret. All that happens in the Wiccan closed circle is secret too. That is also our heritage and tradition. A fan of eclectic, fusion paganism I might be, but tradition still matters in some things.

London's Stone Circle
Saturday, 2 February, 2013

I am standing in a stone circle in a public park overlooking London, with my husband. We hold hands through gloves. Our coats are done up and our woolly hats are pulled over our ears, but still a bitter wind blows through the skeletal trees that surround the stones and makes our eyes water and cheeks tingle. A shaft of sunlight breaks through the grey clouds, making the grass look greener and the stones brighter. It is Imbolc, not yet Valentine's Day, but this cold Saturday afternoon in a park on a south London hill is filled with romance for us, because this is where we were handfasted several summers ago.

Many people are surprised to learn that London has a stone circle. It isn't ancient, like Stonehenge or Avebury. It was built for the millennium celebrations and inaugurated at the spring equinox 2000.

Back in 1997 a group of artists came up with the idea to create a new stone circle for the new millennium. The community got behind the project and gained permission to build it on Hilly Fields – a public park in South London that had been the site of an annual midsummer fair for a quarter of a century.

The inauguration was very much a community event too, multicultural as well as multifaith. Local musicians – including a steel band – provided music, children from the nearby school put on a performance. The stones were blessed by the parish vicar as well as being meaningful to pagans.

It felt right that the inauguration was held at the spring equinox, the time of balance when the day and night are of equal length. At the time I hoped that honouring balance would work its magic to bring about a time of spiritual harmony between those of all faiths and cultures in this great city.

Things have changed a little since then – for the better in my opinion. There is a lovely cafe overlooking the stones now. It sells delicious home-made fare. Today, my husband and I take refuge there from the biting wind. The place is busy – not a table free, but a couple with a young baby in a pram smile at us and gesture that we can take the spare chairs at their table.

We look out at the stones through the cafe window while we sip our hot lattes and eat sweet, moist carrot cake. We watch three little girls wearing brightly coloured boots, coats and hats play hopscotch in the middle of the circle. The children are all from different ethnicities and they play happily together.

The cafe has two large boards for community notices. Next to a big poster saying 'Save Our Hospital' I spot adverts for yoga and meditation classes, Reiki healing and other things that, while not specifically pagan, are definitely in the mind, body and spirit category.

Yet to me the word 'pagan' means more than just a description of those who follow a polytheistic religion such as Wicca. To me being pagan means honouring the spirit of the place. Those who honour that spirit do so here by their love of the place itself. They might be Christians, Muslims, Hindus or atheists, but they honour this place as somewhere the community can meet, play, share food and share good company. And, of course, it is also used from time to time by modern pagans for rituals, such as my own handfasting.

London's stone circle is no relic of the long-lost past, built by long-forgotten pagans for a reason that is shrouded in mystery and whose rituals we can only attempt to reconstruct and revive.

This is a stone circle for this millennium, built by the community to bring the community together. This, to me, is what paganism should be about.

The Druids of Primrose Hill

Sunday, 3 February, 2013

A crowd has gathered in the Hawthorn Grove on Primrose Hill, part of Regent's Park, to celebrate Imbolc with the Loose Association of Druids. Such ceremonies have been traditional here since 1792, when the antiquarian Iolo Morganwg performed a public druidic ritual to attempt to revive the ancient ceremonies performed by our distant ancestors on the most prominent point on the north bank of the Thames.

I'm unsure how many people would have gathered on Primrose Hill to celebrate Imbolc in antiquity, but the crowd today seems pretty large considering it is, once again, cold and blustery. According to Jeremy Morgan, who is group organiser and co-celebrant in this rite, outdoor rituals are popular in the warm weather, but not so much at the coldest time of the year. Spring might be just around the corner, but winter isn't giving up the fight yet.

I take the large crowd as yet another sign that paganism is on the rise in London. There are people here of all ages and seemingly from all walks of life. Many are locals, but a few have travelled a long way – including one young man who was risking missing his flight home to Germany, due to take off from Heathrow Airport just an hour or so after the ritual's end.

Although I have never been to this meeting before, I am made to feel welcome and it is a lovely ritual. We are given printed booklets containing the ceremony so we can all take part. There are poetic words, song, dance and feasting. The feasting is a central part – people have brought home-made cakes as well as warming ginger wine and flasks of hot coffee.

After the feast we are given gifts – a nut and sprig of heather

– as symbols of nature's blessings. I leave feeling the warmth of new friendships despite the cold weather and I promise to come back again.

Yet the day is not without a problem – and it is one that is an issue in all of contemporary paganism. When we arrived at the Hawthorn Grove we discovered that others had been using it the night before – with little respect for the environment. We found the remains of a camp fire, even though fires are banned in Regent's Park. We also found a circle marked out in flour on the grass. It could have been worse. At least flour is biodegradable and doesn't cause long-term damage to plants.

All the pagan groups I know are environmentally conscious. Paganism is a nature religion. We want to save the Earth, not harm her. Most pagans make sure to leave only their footprints at sacred sites, yet often have to clear up litter when they arrive.

I am convinced that most of those who leave behind candle stubs, floral tributes and such things as rings of flour on the ground do so in ignorance. Obviously, anyone can do what they like in their own back gardens, but in a public place one person's sacred offerings are just a mess of rubbish to those who want to enjoy the space afterwards. In London, there are a lot of people wanting to share and enjoy those same spaces.

As I said before, most pagans are ethical about their activities, but as paganism increases we need to face up to the problems of what to do about those few who are not.

I Went Across London to a Moot with No Name ...
Monday, 4 February, 2013
Tonight I am at a moot with no name – The Moot with No Name as it has come to be called.

Back in Anglo-Saxon times a moot – or 'folkmoot' – was a meeting of people who lived in an area to discuss important matters. It was a type of community government where members of the tribe – or perhaps just the elders – could have their say and make decisions about local issues. It often took place in a building called a moot hall or on an ancient mound designated as a moot hill.

Today the term is used to mean a meeting where pagans get together to talk about stuff and usually takes place in a pub. The discussions are more about topics of esoteric interest than decisions about any type of government. To be honest, modern-day pagans don't really want to be governed, and trying to get a bunch of pagans to agree on anything can be like flogging a dead horse.

But pagans – particularly in London it seems – do like to get together at moots to socialise, chat, discuss things (even if they are never going to agree), listen to talks by eminent speakers and (quite often) heckle them afterwards. Usually this is done in a friendly way, where those who disagree agree to differ and everyone enjoys the banter. Sometimes it is more divisive. Sometimes groups splinter and go off to form their own moot.

An important Central London pagan moot of recent times was Talking Stick, which began at The Plough pub on Wednesday, 14th February, 1990. After many years the group split into two. At the time I am writing this, we have Secret Chiefs, which meets at the Devereux, in Holborn, on alternate Mondays, and The Moot with No Name, which meets at The Bell, in Aldgate, on alternate Mondays.

There are more. Wherever you are in London – east, south, west, north or centre – you can find a moot nearby. There are general pagan moots and ones aimed at those of specific traditions or specialist interests, from heathenism to BDSM. Is this diversification a good thing, or a bad thing? Personally, I like the fact I now have more events to go to. But, of course, sometimes groups divide on less than happy terms.

At tonight's moot, at The Moot with No Name, Miguel Rowlanes is talking about What Cernunnos Means to Me. A pagan for over 20 years and having followed traditions, 'From

Ancient Mexican ways to OTO to Wicca to OBOD,' Miguel says he enjoys meeting people and having discussions. That's what moots are all about, after all.

Miguel is here to talk about Cernunnos, the antlered god of the animals and wild places, whose image is seen on some of the oldest works of pagan art. Cernunnos is Miguel's personal deity. He first encountered the Celtic god after inheriting a set of stag antlers from an old man in Suffolk, when he himself was a child. He talks about meeting Cernunnos through shamanic journeys with traditional practitioners in Mexico, through the sexual rites of the *Ordo Templi Orientis* (OTO), through Wicca's seasonal celebrations of the Goddess and the God and through druidic rites in the woods. Yet the message he sums up with is that while we might all do things in different ways, and call our gods and goddesses by different names, there is no need to fight among ourselves.

And, Miguel says, in the pagan community today, peace and healing are what we need. His voice has the weight of an elder; the weight of experience. For once, everyone at the moot agrees and there is no heckling.

Walking in the Footsteps of London's Pagan Luminaries
Tuesday, 5 February, 2013

London has been home to many of contemporary paganism's major figures. Gerald Gardner, the founder of modern Wicca, moved to London in the 1940s. Ross Nichols, who founded the Order of Bards, Ovates and Druids, was the headmaster of a London school at around the same time. Other former inhabitants of occult London include Elizabethan astrologer John Dee; visionary artist William Blake; founder of the Theosophical Society, Helena Blavatsky; founder of Thelema, Aleister Crowley; precursor of chaos magic Austin Osman Spare, and master of weirdness Kenneth Grant.

Tonight I am at a talk called Kenneth Grant: Dracula's Tantric

Rituals. I am at Treadwell's bookshop and the speaker is esoteric writer Alistair Coombs. Alistair described Kenneth Grant as, 'The most original occultist of the twentieth century.' Grant worked with Crowley during the older man's final days and was a friend of Spare. He formed the Typhonian Order – which developed out of the OTO – and was seriously into sex magic. Grant fused Crowley's Thelema with Tantra and, Coombs says, 'also combined this with ideas from witchcraft, including the importance of the feminine and the Kali and lunar cycles.'

Many of Grant's most famous books were originally published in the 1970s, when weirdness was counterculture high fashion. He blended occult traditions with material from science fiction and horror. He saw stories and the imagination as an important part of magic.

Although that concept is one I agree with, my background is Wiccan and Grant's system is an area I know little about. The talk is fascinating, but I come away realising I have a gap in my knowledge. I need to read up on it – and London is the place to do that.

Central London has four major esoteric and pagan book stores. Two are in Bloomsbury, near the British Museum; they are Treadwell's, in Store Street, and Atlantis Bookshop, in Museum Street. Two are in Covent Garden: Watkins Books, in Cecil Court, and Mysteries, in Monmouth Street.

The oldest is Watkins, which opened in 1897. Atlantis Bookshop was established in 1922, Mysteries opened in 1982 on the crest of the New Age wave, while Treadwell's was originally in Covent Garden, moving to its current home in 2011. If you can't find the tome or Tarot deck you are looking for in one of those places, you will struggle to find it anywhere.

The store owners are also a mine of useful information, whether you are starting out in the Craft or are an experienced practitioner. The shops have meeting rooms as well, with schedules of talks and workshops on a wide variety of subjects, like the one tonight.

Visit the older shops and know that your feet are walking in the footsteps of Crowley, Spare, Gardner, Nichols, Grant and other occult and pagan luminaries of the past. Attend an event at any of them and know you will meet the occult and pagan luminaries of today. Browse the bookshelves and I am sure you will find a book that is calling out to you.

A Time for Healing, Communication and Growth
Wednesday, 6 February, 2013

I light a candle; I say some words as I watch the flame glow within a chalice of healing. I send the energy to a friend who has asked for help through the internet. I am at home in London, where I work from my computer, writing this chapter and connected via the internet with other pagans all over the world.

Again via the internet I read an invitation to a spiritual healing group meet-up in the centre of London tonight. I am tempted, but it will probably do me more good to stay at home and rest.

As I have said, London is a melting pot – or a cauldron – of magical ideas and, right now, I believe London is in the springtime of a Golden Age of paganism, spirituality and magic. I could go to an event every night of the week if I wanted to. There are often several talks, workshops, moots and meet-ups in different parts of London at the same time.

But, through the internet, we are all connected wherever we are and ideas can be shared through pagan networks, blogs and other social media. There is also Paganradio.co.uk, which broadcasts many of the talks from London moots so that they can be enjoyed by everyone. That springtime of a Golden Age of paganism isn't just happening in London, I know. It is happening all over England, Europe, America and Australia. And it is growing.

A Very Modern King Arthur

Steve Andrews

Arthur Uther Pendragon used to be John Timothy Rothwell before he came to the realisation of who he really was and changed his name by deed poll in June, 1986. He claims to be the reincarnated and modern King Arthur who has returned, as the prophesy foretold would happen, when Britain was in its time of greatest need. He is an eco-warrior, activist and leader of a Druid Order known as the Loyal Arthurian Warband.

Of course Arthur realises that many people will think that his claims are outrageous and so he often introduces himself as the "nutter who thinks he is King Arthur." If you want to accept him as a king that's great but if not then that is fine with him too.

People always ask me how I got involved with Arthur in the first place and it's a good question. It may well be that I knew him way back in the Dark Ages and was one of his knights then, but if so I don't remember it so I'll explain how I came to meet him in this life.

It happened something like this: I was an avid networker in the global underground, made up of countless fanzines and small press publications, including poets, DJs, musicians, writers and activists. Also, being a singer-songwriter, freelance writer and poet myself, I like to find homes for my creative output and have found this method invaluable.

I had come upon an address for the Loyal Arthurian Warband newsletter in a FIN (Free Information Newsletter) and thought I'd get in touch, so I sent an introductory letter, publicity materials and SAE to them. I used to do a lot of this sort of thing and knew that sometimes you got speedy replies, which can lead on into new and exciting friendships or outlets for your work, and other times you hear no more. It can be very hit or miss but this adds to the thrill and appeal of it all.

I think about six weeks had passed and I'd forgotten all about it but I happened to be the guest musician on a local radio programme presented by Steve Johnson for Red Dragon FM Radio. The name of the show was to prove very significant indeed but this I was to learn the day after the actual broadcast. The programme was called "The Round Table" and I was on the pre-Christmas edition, which went out on the 23rd of December.

All went well on air and I did a few seasonal songs and chatted with my host who actually asked me about any recent success I'd had from all my letter writing. This too was of significance but I didn't realise this then.

Well, we finished the show eventually and I returned home but the next morning, which was Christmas Eve, brought a welcome surprise in the post. Normally I get lots of mail with loads of replies from all my networking efforts and suchlike. Of course at such a time of year you can expect the postman to be struggling with a heavy mailbag but all that arrived that particular morning was a solitary letter. The letter, however, was from King Arthur himself.

I lost no time in opening my single piece of Christmas mail that morning and read with interest what Arthur had to say. I was quite excited at having had a letter from a real king. This letter, I thought, was worthy of being called "Royal Mail!"

King Arthur briefly described the different degrees of knighthood in his order and went on to tell me that a good way to find out more was to tune in to a documentary soon to be aired on Radio 4. I made a mental connection to the radio show I had just been on, and I do have a personal interest in and belief that synchronicities like this are some form of signpost system for us to pay heed to.

The day of the broadcast arrived and I put a cassette in my hi-fi to record the show too. I sat down and listened attentively to what was on. Not far into the documentary, I was pleasantly surprised to hear the voice of a very good friend of mine, who is commonly known as Pixi, and he was wishing everyone at Twyford Down a "Happy Beltane." These words summed up nicely the very jolly and pagan flavour of the documentary and I was all ears.

The rest of the programme followed Arthur on his quest to get to Stonehenge for the summer solstice and was a very informative and enjoyable piece of radio detailing the adventures of the King and his followers. It includes a bit about a bunch of squatters from the ranks of Arthur's order, whom he left behind with instructions to occupy Winchester Cathedral in protest at the authorities stopping druids from attending their cathedral at Stonehenge.

This story in itself, as an example of the King and the Warband in action, appealed to my sense of adventure as well as making a very good point. After hearing the documentary and after finding that I already had some personal connection with the King and his druid order via Pixi, I decided that I definitely should get far more involved and I wrote and told King Arthur my decision.

Before I go any further, I feel that I ought to tell you a little about Pixi so here goes: I first came upon him when he was sixteen and had run away from home and school for various personal reasons. He had been living in a squat and I had recently gained myself the tenancy of a Cardiff council house where I was living with my son, Isaac, who at that time was a toddler. Somehow or other several of the squatters ended up living 'unofficially' at my house and one of the first to do this was Pixi, who then went under his real name of Neill Morgan.

Neill lived at my house off and on for many years and went through many changes as well as venturing off into all sorts of adventures in the big wide world. His name he always insisted was spelt with a double 'l' and once under the influence of acid he decided to change it to 'Reill,' which he claimed was pronounced like "real." He had already created a home-tattoo on his arm spelling out his name but he cut into this to alter it to "Reill" and still bears the scars to this day.

Crazy behaviour, or a young man several years ahead of Richey Edwards from the Manic Street Preachers, who in the band's heyday before his mysterious disappearance once carved "4 Real" into his arm? Maybe Pixi was a real-life original Manic Street Preacher before the band had even formed?

He was a colourful, charismatic character and an obvious entertainer from the start. Pixi soon started to learn guitar and to play all sorts of songs including some he penned himself. One of these songs was called Chameleon and contained the very aptly descriptive lines: "Some people call me Chameleon, They say I change from face to face, But they don't know me, They don't know me at all."

One of Pixi's life-styles was that of the so-called New Age traveller, and to give him his dues on this, this way of life was something he has often returned to and he spent time living with a group who carry all their worldly goods in handcarts. But before this Pixi had also learned several other musical instruments like the mandolin and penny whistle and had become an accomplished busker as well as a talented singer-songwriter. And he looked the part; a real raggle-taggle gypsy look with well-worn hippy-style clothes, piercings and dreadlocks. So it was no great surprise to find that he had ended up as a 'Bard' of the Loyal Arthurian Warband or as Arthur's "Herald" at Twyford Down road protest camp.

As it happened, my friend Pixi was back in Cardiff at the time the BBC Radio 4 programme went out on air and I told him all about it when I next saw him. In the time that had elapsed between the recording of the documentary and now a lot had changed in his life again, and he had forgotten all about it until I jogged his memory. Soon after this, I received another letter from King Arthur offering me a commission to be knighted into the

Warband as any one of the degrees of knighthood I considered right for me and also, I was to extend this offer to Pixi.

Apparently Sky TV had approached Arthur with a view to making a programme about reincarnation in which they wanted to feature him and a bit about his supporters. If Pixi and I so desired we could be publicly knighted at a suitable location of our choosing, to be included in the finished documentary.

I knew that all this seemed right for me, and also, that I was happy to take on the titles of "Quest Knight and Bard" to the Loyal Arthurian Warband. I was already a bard, being a poet, singer-songwriter and performer, and Quest Knight too felt suitable because I see life as a quest in any case. I had no knowledge of a past life with Arthur so couldn't resume my "true and former name" as a Shield Knight but I do believe in reincarnation and agreed with what his order stands for, so this is what I told him.

Pixi too agreed to take the same titles, and we settled on Tinkinswood Burial Chamber as the chosen location where the ceremony would take place. There has been a certain magical thread running through this story so far, a mystical connection, and both Pixi and I have a great affinity for the site we had chosen, having spent a lot of time there in the past. We had often gone there for a bit of an outdoor party, as well as for more serious contemplation and it is a place that is very popular with local pagans, set as it is in a tranquil field a few miles out of the bustling city. It was to be another such party but one that is not easily forgotten!

On the day in question, which was in February 1996, there was a knock on my door and it was Arthur who had arrived with the Sky TV crew. He told me then that he hadn't slept for three days and I mention this because it has a lot of bearing on his character and what makes him my idea of a Celtic battle chieftain. Anyway, we had to go into Cardiff city centre to collect Pixi and other supporters that wanted to come along. Sky TV paid the taxi fare for them to get to Tinkinswood.

When we got to the location the TV crew wanted to film Arthur making his way across the field to the ancient site and this they did. He was dressed in his druid robe and a cape and carrying his "Holy Lance", a wooden staff with copper wire wound around it and a massive quartz crystal at the end. He looked the part!

The knighting ceremony went well and Pixi and I emerged from a hole in the burial chamber to meet Arthur on the grass outside. The idea was to symbolise being born again as knights. We both swore by the sword Excalibur to uphold the Ancient Virtues of Truth, Honour and Justice, and yes, Arthur has a sword with the same name as the one in the legends and how he came upon it is a story in itself.

Eventually the cameramen had enough footage and had recorded all they needed for their forthcoming documentary so they bade us goodbye. Arthur, who had already drunk some cider or "Druid Fluid" as he calls it, signalled to Pixi to pass the homemade wine or "Pixi Piss" as he called it and glugged some of that back.

In a short time he looked conspicuously out of it and ended up unconscious on the muddy grass. Now this could have appeared to have been because he couldn't handle his drink but, as I knew, it was actually because he had been without sleep for days.

There was nothing we could do but wait for him to wake up and be able to make his way back across the fields. Pixi went off and collected some brushwood and soon had a small fire going and he entertained us with more songs on his guitar as the skies grew dark. My hands were too cold to play.

Eventually Arthur woke up and we all made our way back to the road and walked the short way to the outskirts of Saint Nicholas village. The problem was how we were all going to get back to Cardiff without any transport. We were a motley crew very out of keeping with the houses and types of people who lived in the quiet countryside hamlet. There were five of us left including Arthur, and there were two guitars, a mandolin and all of us were dressed in colourful clothing.

Pixi tried knocking on the door of one of the houses to explain our predicament and was told that the house owner would order a taxi. We carried on sitting on a low wall but in vain because no cab arrived.

A man from the village came past us walking his dog and our problem was explained to him. He said he would phone a taxi too but this time we were in luck because one arrived. The only trouble now was that the driver said there were too many to be allowed in the car.

Again, Pixi was the hero of the story because he volunteered to walk and hitch back to Ely where I lived. Arthur gave him the Holy Lance and said that its magic would help Pixi get back. We all got in the taxi and were soon back at my house warming up.

Imagine everyone's surprise when 10 minutes' later there was a bang on the door. It was Pixi who said that he had walked the short stretch up to Cowbridge to Cardiff Road and held up the staff to the first car that came along. The driver stopped and gave him a lift right to the bottom of the road I lived in. The magic had certainly worked!

Being a druid and friend of King Arthur has given me some really memorable experiences and shown me why he is deserving of his title. I used to be a member of the Gurdjieff Work many years ago and came upon the idea of "Super Effort". Gurdjieff explained it with the following example: walking from A to B using Super Effort would mean you walk from the start point to your destination, then return again to A and once more walk to B. Only then have you completed the walk.

Arthur is the only person I know whom I can say I have seen employ such persistence and perseverance on a course, and I once told him that he uses this power and ability that Gurdjieff had spoken of. But here is another story about him that shows why I thought like this:

It was a very wet Samhain afternoon when Arthur arrived at my house unexpectedly. "I have a quest I would like you to accompany me on," he said. He went on to explain that it involved going down to West Wales to a sacred mountain near Newport known as Carn Ingli where a man called Laurence Main wanted to be knighted and to become a member of the Loyal Arthurian Warband.

Laurence is an interesting character in his own right being an expert on sacred sites and ancient footpaths around the country. He had been living on the peak of Carn Ingli as the Welsh Saint Brynach had once done back in the fifth century, and like Arthur had donned the role of the Celtic king, Laurence had taken on the mantle of the holy man from the past.

He was involved in what was known as the Dragon Project and was compiling the dream narratives of people who spent the night in his company on Carn Ingli. They would sleep in a tent and Laurence would wait for his guest to show REM sleep, and would wake them and ask them to record what they had been dreaming about into his tape recorder.

But back to my house in Ely where I noticed that Arthur was limping and his leg was bandaged up. He told me that he had been in an accident earlier that day when he was knocked off his motorbike, but undeterred and having promised he would be at Carn Ingli had hired a car which was what we would be using to get there.

The weather was atrocious but I had nothing else planned and being a Quest Knight now thought I would join Arthur on this one. We set off through the torrential rain and hoped it would have stopped by the time we reached our destination. We were in luck and after stopping off to get some basic supplies we found the mountain and parked the car. I went on ahead because Arthur was struggling due to his bad leg.

I will never forget meeting Laurence who came down to greet

us. He had a massive bushy white beard, dreadlocks and was barefoot even though it was freezing cold and the end of October. Laurence really is like a holy man of the mountains!

We made our way up to a flat space where he had his camp and two tents. We had just got settled when we were joined by a woman called Emma who lived in a farm down below and Megan, a young lady from Nova Scotia who had been hitch-hiking and was trying to get to Ireland. There are ferries from the nearby Fishguard but she hadn't got that far.

It was getting dark and colder and Emma asked Megan if she wanted to come on back down to the farmhouse but amazingly this young woman from Canada chose to stay up on the mountain with a Bard, a Holy Man and a King!

Laurence was knighted and after sharing some food and drink it was decided that we would retire for the night into the shelter of the tents. I had already expressed an interest in the dream project and it was an ideal opportunity for me to be the dreamer. I joined Laurence in his tent and Arthur and Megan took the other.

I was unable to get comfortable or to get to sleep. The ground was rocky and although I had a sleeping bag I was too cold. Every so often Laurence would ask me if I had been dreaming yet and I would say that no, I still hadn't got to sleep. As the night went forward though and I was tossing and turning in a vain effort to drift off, I suddenly had a mental vision and I told my companion who switched on his tape recorder.

I said that I had seen three black cloaked figures and a hill like Glastonbury Tor. That was it. It wasn't a dream but the best I could come up with. Eventually after failing to get any sleep and a terrible night, the light of dawn was spreading through the canvas and I thought I might as well get up. I opened the tent flap and crawled outside.

Arthur was doing the same and bid me good morning. He went on to tell me he had been awake all night too, in his case because he had been fighting "psychic battles". Arthur said that Ring-wraiths, the evil beings from the Tolkien Lord of the Rings story, had been coming for Megan and he had been defending her from them.

This wasn't such a shock to me and didn't sound crazy because I had experienced the black-clothed figures in my vision. I told Arthur about this and we concluded that I had seen the same entities. Arthur went on to add that he thought Tolkien had tapped into a reality but expressed it as fiction.

Eventually it was fully light and Megan and Laurence had got up too. We said our goodbyes and Arthur and I made our way back to the car down in the valley.

A short while after we pulled into a garage because Arthur wanted to get some cigarettes. He said to me: "Steve, you see that woman in the shop, well, if I tell her who I am and what we have just been doing, that I am King Arthur and that you are a bard, and we have been on a sacred mountain with a Welsh saint where I have been fighting psychic battles with evil characters from a book by J.R.R. Tolkien that were trying to attack a young woman from Canada, and that now we are driving back to Cardiff where I will be knighting a man who works for the BBC (Peter, one of the main members of the team behind the series The Slate, was due to be going under the sword), she will think I am nuts. She won't believe a word of it but you will know that it is the truth!"

Indeed, I did know that it was all true. Of course, Arthur didn't tell the woman at the counter any of that and we left her none the wiser before the drive back to Cardiff. For him this was just another day and what could be expected in the life of King Arthur in the modern world.

Canadian Paganism – Turn and Face the North!

Brendan Myers

To begin with, Canada is a very big country. We have the second-biggest back yard in the whole world. At the same time we are also a small country: with only around 33 million people, we are one-tenth the size of America, half the size of Britain and France, and around one-third the size of Germany. Around 20,000 of us are pagans, and we have just as much diversity of path and tradition as you may find in any other country's pagan world. Furthermore, being so very big, with cities that are like islands of civilization surrounded by oceans of prairie or mountain or shield-land, local pagan movements in Canada are often sadly isolated from each other. Thus a definitive statement of 'Canadian' paganism perhaps cannot be written. Being so diverse, and distant from each other, it might not be possible to attribute a distinct cultural and spiritual character to all Canadian pagans as a whole, in the way that could be done for the pagans of, let's say, San Francisco. And yet Canadians do have a distinct society. We are not just Americans who live in a colder country. We are certainly not 'North Americans' – that phrase denotes a continent, not a people. We are Canadians. We were created as a nation by a treaty, not by a war. And we were created through the collaboration of numerous communities: French, English, Scottish, Irish, and hundreds of Aboriginal First Nations. We are fiscally conservative and yet socially and culturally liberal. We discovered insulin, invented the telephone, and UN peace-keeping. The Canadian Dream involves "peace, order, and good government", with a continental railway and a national public health system. We are peace-loving, compassionate, and cooperative, except perhaps when we play hockey.

We are religious (14 million of us are Catholic, for instance), but religion has almost no place in our political landscape. We are curiously religious and secular at the same time. And we love our home and native land, the true north strong and free.

I've experienced pagan culture in six of Canada's ten provinces, as well as a number of European countries. It appears to me that there are, indeed, a few features of the Canadian pagan scene that are similar across the country, and that one might not find in other countries, or at least not to the same degree. For instance, we have a different wheel of the year. At Beltaine, in most of the country, it makes no sense to celebrate the return of the springtime, because we may still be up to our knees in snow. Nor is Samhain the end of summer, because in most of the country, the summer ended at the autumnal equinox, six weeks earlier. And with a territory as large as ours, other correspondences on the wheel of the year necessarily vary from one region to the next. But there is one constant in many Canadian pagan circles, from sea to sea. We had a western frontier in colonial times, like America did, but we also had a *northern* frontier. And our frontiers were never 'conquered' or 'won'. They were *explored,* and (with a few exceptions) they were settled peacefully. In fact our northern frontier is still being explored, and in many ways it remains a land of mystery and discovery. The experience is perhaps comparable to what Europeans felt centuries ago, before the discovery of our continent, when they faced the Atlantic Ocean. So when we cast a circle, and turn to face the north, we find ourselves facing a realm of the unknown, one-tenth the size of our planet. It is a realm of terrifying loneliness, but also majestic beauty.

(By the way: the North West Passage? It's ours. Just a friendly reminder.)

Canadian pagans also tend to be well educated and well read. A survey conducted by Sian Reid, then a professor of sociology at Carleton University, found that around 30 per cent of Canadian pagans had some level of college or university education. This was 10 per cent more than the rate of higher education among the Canadian population as a whole. A case in point is the Gaia Gathering, Canada's national pagan conference. It was founded by professional academics, and it moves to a different university each year. It always includes an academic stream where professors and grad students present their work, and in most cases the special guest speaker is also an academic. Canadian pagans generally do *not* hold the view that "book learning" is useless, or inferior to personal experience, or somehow a corrupting influence. Reason and gnosis tend to be held in equal esteem. Educated pagans are not scorned for 'elitism' but respected for their knowledge and intellectual achievements. Nor is formal education the only criteria here. Since at least the mid 1990s, Canadian pagans have had a tradition of honouring and respecting Elders: something we learned from local Aboriginal people. These knowledgeable and experienced individuals have helped build and guide their communities for half a century or more, and receive as much respect, if not more, than our academics.

Another distinct feature of Canadian paganism has to do with the way we express our moral values. As in other countries, the Wiccan Rede is usually the statement of morality that Canadian pagans turn to first. But in Canada one hears the language of responsibility, cooperation, and community-building, just as often as one hears the language of personal freedom. These ideas are also readily put into practice. For instance, the Pagan Hot Showers network, which helps people find accommodation and various services while travelling, was created by a Canadian: Jean-Marc Ladouceur. The moral language of heroic virtue, whether from the Triads of Ireland, or the Eddas and Sagas, or the Seven Grandfathers of the Algonquin, also has great promi-nence in the Canadian pagan moral discourse. There are many lists of the pagan virtues, but the fact that such lists are being used right alongside the Rede seems distinctly Canadian. I've never encountered it to the same extent elsewhere. Canadians also started using such lists about a decade or so before they were popularised in America by groups like ADF, and The Ring of Troth. Canadian pagans can be just as individualist as anyone else, but we also understand that our very individuality is embedded in a social world, which grants the individual her possibilities. Indeed, at a panel talk a recent Gaia Gathering which I attended, one participant described the American emphasis on individualism and personal freedom as 'libertarian paranoia', and as 'the fear of other people, even including other pagans.'

This leads to a third feature of the Canadian pagan scene: our multiculturalism. Canada was the first nation in the world to make multiculturalism into a government policy, and we see this reflected in the diversity of pagan paths at our festivals and gatherings. In western Quebec and eastern Ontario, for instance, most pagan public events are fully bilingual: English and French. And across the country, one is likely to find people who practice more than one path at the same time. Eclectic pagans are sometimes accused of being unfocused or superficial. Canadian pagans have learned to make eclecticism into a way to accept each other's differences, and also communicate, teach, learn, and share new ideas. It is no accident that Canada's largest pagan camping festival is called 'Kaleidoscope Gathering'. Our pagan movement is itself a kaleidoscope of many colours, and many paths.

Naturally, with a country as geographically large and culturally diverse as Canada, there are exceptions to everything I've written here. There is also much more that could be said, that I lack the space to say. But I hope that this little introduction shows that the Canadian pagan movement is alive and flourishing. Our events and festivals are as enjoyable and magical as any you'll find elsewhere in the world. Our writers, teachers and leaders are just as capable, creative, and as wise as their more famous counterparts in other countries. After decades in the shadow of the big personalities and organisations from Britain and America, Canadians are doing it for ourselves – indeed we have been doing it for ourselves all along – and what we are doing is quite amazing. Come and visit – you'll see!

A few leading Canadian personalities:

Maryanne Pearce and Austin Lawrence. (Ottawa, Ontario) Austin is an Asatru Gothi, and Maryanne's path emerges from her Celtic and Mohawk ancestors. Together, they are the directors of Raven's Knoll, a 100-acre special events campground near Eganville, Ontario, and also the directors of Kaleidoscope Gathering, Canada's largest pagan festival. As such, Austin and Maryanne are among Canada's most important community organisers. Always insisting that the land belongs to the community and not to themselves (although they are the financially responsible deed holders), they work hard all year round to foster a pagan community that is welcoming, inclusive, celebratory, and fun.
Web site: http://ravensknoll.ca

Richard and Tamarra James. (Toronto, Ontario) Originally from Vancouver, when they came to Toronto they founded a local organisation called The Wiccan Church of Canada, which has held weekly open rituals and open teaching sessions since 1979. They also founded their own Wiccan tradition, called the Odyssean tradition, which marries BTW influences with Greek mythology and original contributions. This tradition, and the WCC organization, is almost certainly the most influential force in pagan thinking and practice in south-western and central Ontario. The James' also hold Gerald Gardner's library, having purchased it from Ripley's Museum, and they make it available to researchers from time to time.
Web site: http://www.wcc.on.ca

Lucie DuFresne (Ottawa, Ontario) is a lecturer in anthropology, women's studies, and theology at the University of Ottawa. Through her personal mentoring work, and the courses she teaches at the university, it is likely that she influences the spiritual life of over a thousand people every year.
Web site: N/a.

The Dragon Ritual Drummers (Niagara Falls, Ontario) are a popular pagan musical group. Influenced primarily by Voodoo and Santaria, a DRD concert is always a wild, energetic and empowering experience.
http://www.dragonritualdrummers.com/

Meri Fowler (Montreal, Quebec) is a palliative care nurse, a Ninjutsu instructor, and the director of the Avalon Centre, a large pagan community centre on Montreal's West Island. The centre features two ritual spaces, a dojo, a healing centre, and a library. She is also the founder of a home-grown path of Wicca called the Greenwood Tradition, which has hundreds of practitioners.
http://www.avalonnaturel.com/

Sandra and Vanessa Smith (Halifax, Nova Scotia) are the mother/daughter team who run Little Mysteries, a pagan book and supply store in Halifax, Nova Scotia. Staff and volunteers also use the store as a teaching centre and special events venue.
http://www.littlemysteries.com/

Shelley Rabinovitch (Ottawa, Ontario) is also a lecturer in cultural anthropology at the University of Ottawa, and the author of the first ethnographic study of Canadian pagans ever undertaken. She has published several books including *An Ye Harm None: Magical Morality and Modern Ethics*, and *The Encyclopedia of Witchcraft*.
http://www.cla-srs.uottawa.ca/eng/faculty/rabinovitch.html

Sam Wagar (Vancouver, BC) is a widely published writer, and the founder of several pagan organisations including the Gathering for Life on Earth (Western Canada's largest pagan and alternative spirituality festival), and the Congregationalist Wiccan Association. His influence sometimes appears invisible, as he tends to turn the leadership of his projects over to others once they are established and running smoothly. As a teacher, he has directly or indirectly influenced as many as half of all the pagans in British Columbia.
Web site: n/a.

Fritz Muntean (Vancouver, BC) is a co-founder of the influential NROOGD tradition of California, a Masters degree holder in Religious Studies, and (until 2003) he was the editor of The Pomegranate, an academic journal of pagan studies. It is likely that 90 per cent of all the pagans in British Columbia were trained directly or indirectly by either Fritz Muntean or by Sam Wagar, or by both of them together.
Web site: n/a.

Arin Murphy-Hiscock (Montreal, Quebec) plays the cello in a local symphony, and teaches at the Crescent Moon School of Magic and Paganism. Her books include *Power Spellcraft for Life*, *The Way of the Green Witch*, and *Pagan Pregnancy: A Spiritual Journey from Maiden to Mother*.
http://www.arinmurphyhiscock.com

Scarlet Jory (Montreal, Quebec) is the owner of Melange Magique/The Magical Blend, a successful occult store in Montreal. She is also the founder and principal teacher of The Crescent Moon School of Magic and Paganism, also based in Montreal.
http://www.mtl-magicalcircle.ca/

Kerr CuChullain (Surrey, BC), is a recipient of the Governor General's Exemplary Service Medal for his many years as a police officer in Vancouver. He has worked for social justice for pagans in Canada and around the world, by investigating hate crimes against pagans, and also publishing his discoveries in various books and in hundreds of articles. His books include *The Law Enforcement Guide to Wicca*, *Witch Hunts* and *Full Contact Magick*. A former Preceptor-General of the Officers of Avalon, an organisation which represents pagans in police, fire, and EMT services, he is also the founder and head of a pagan knighthood organisation called The Order of Scathach.
http://kerrcuhulain.blogspot.com/

Amanda Hyde (Hamilton, Ontario) is the regional coordinator for all the Pagan Pride Day events in Canada. She also manages the PPD for her own city, Hamilton, which in its fourth year was the largest single-day pagan event on the continent.
http://www.ppdhamilton.org/

Brendan Myers (Elora, Ontario) is a professor of philosophy, and the author of hundreds of articles and six influential books, including *A Pagan Testament*, *Loneliness and Revelation*, and the award-winning treatment of mythology and ethics, *The Other Side of Virtue*. He's also known in his local area as a songwriter and Bardic performer, and he co-hosts "Standing Stone and Garden Gate", a popular pagan podcast.
http://brendanmyers.net

Robin Skelton (Victoria, BC) began his life in Yorkshire, England, served as a sergeant in the Royal Air Force in India, but quickly found his calling as a professor of English and creative writing. A prolific writer and a true polymath, he wrote more than 50 books of poetry, fifteen nonfiction books, edited 24 anthologies, and published various memoirs, novels, and translations. Skelton died in 1997, at the age of 72.

Canadian Pagan Internet Resources, Podcasts, and Blogs

Wicca from a Canadian Perspective – http://thewicca.ca
The Wiccan Web: An Online Community - http://wiccanweb.ca/
The Wigglian Way – http://thewigglianway.ca/
Kakophonos Internet Radio – http://www.kakophonos.com/
Standing Stone and Garden Gate – http://stonegatepodshow,net
Shortening the Road – http://shorteningtheroad.blogspot.com/
Walking the Hedge – http://walkingthehedge.net

Notable Regular Pagan Events and Festivals in Canada

Gaia Gathering / Canadian National Pagan Conference. Usually on the May 24 Long Weekend; location varies.
http://www.gaiagathering.ca/

Wic-Can Fest: near Mansfield, Ontario; usually in mid to late June.
http://www.wiccanfest.com/wiccanfest/index.html

Kaleidoscope Gathering: at Raven's Knoll, near Eganville, Ontario; early August.
http://www.kaleidoscope-gathering.ca/

Pan Fest; near Edmonton, Alberta; usually on the August Long Weekend.
http://www.panfest.ca/

Aegis; near Port Royal, Nova Scotia, usually on the August Long Weekend.
http://www.witchvox.com/vn/vn_detail/dt_ev.html?a=cans&id=62540

Harvest Fest, near Mansfield, Ontario; early October.
http://www.wiccanfest.com/harvestfest/index.html

Gathering for Life on Earth, near Vancouver, BC, usually on the May Long Weekend.
http://www.gatheringforlife.org/

Eclectic Mystic

Shirley LaBoucane

My name is Shirley LaBoucane and I am a Métis Cree from Ontario, Canada and I am a mystic.

When I reflect on my spiritual path I think about how my family influenced me, I recall ceremonies celebrated on a tree-less land where wild winds blew and the fragrance of sweet grass filled the clean crisp air of the prairies. Families and friends gathering to share an ancient wisdom; a society living in harmony and peace with mother earth, a way of life that we believe now will never be forsaken.

You could say my spiritual practices are a direct result of my heritage, my mother was a Cree from Alberta and my father's roots came from Britain. The Cree and the Celtic, two powerful cultures who believed in a holistic approach to life. The ancient Celts and the Aboriginals of North America both cultivated a divine connection with their deities and with their ancestors, between earth, wind and sky they felt the sacredness of life as they drew energies from the hallowed divinity that encompasses us all.

Curling up at night in my bed, my ears listening to my Indian mother's soft mellow voice as she shared her stories of shape shifters and life on the northern plains; often the look in my mother's ebony eyes was wistful as she shared stories about her people, looking back now it was important to her to keep the link with the past alive.

In contrast to my mother's dark eyes were the eyes of my English grandmother. The memory of her clear hazel eyes reminds me of her tales of fairies and a land covered in eerie mists and ancient ghosts; it was through this mystical Celtic woman that my gift of intuition came to me. I watched her as she would tell women the gender of their unborn babies and what colour their hair and eyes would be … I thought her a most wise woman.

So you see when I consider my spirituality I think of it in colours, the red path for my mother's ebony eyes and the emerald path for the hazel eyes of my grandmother.

I practice a philosophy based on the Medicine Wheel and the Celtic Wheel of the Year. Within my ceremonies I ask many beings to pray for me, to gift me with their wisdom. Teachers such as cedar and deer have lessons that can aid me in my journey.

Soft and fair is the morning; Grandfather Sun breathes sweet thoughts everywhere and each morning before I get out of bed I give thanks to Him for my day. This practice nourishes my spirit and helps to set the mood for my day. Sometimes making time for prayer can be difficult, but when I take time to pray and to smudge, the world of the seen and unseen opens for me and sacred truths unfold within me. Grandfather Sun wakes me from the secret world of the subconscious; my mind still fresh from its astral journeys, the beauty of the morning stirs me to morning prayer, Grandmother Moon whispers her farewell as Grandfather Sun makes his entrance, and before the rest of my family begins their day I am smudging, doing my prayers and making an offering of tobacco. This way of life just makes sense to me, it feeds my spirit and connects me to God.

Ritual is so important to me because it is belief in action, burning my sage, offering tobacco these are demonstrations of faith. Ritual opens up pathways of change and creates an atmosphere where I can transform and evolve. The energy created from ceremony is released to the four directions and it is my hope that my prayers can help bring change to this world.

I welcome the presence of the angels, spirits of the plants and animals for they bring joy and much needed guidance to my day; at sunset I stop and whisper a prayer of thanks for the cloud of protection that all my relations: the winged ones, the four legged, the two legged and the creepers and crawlers have bestowed upon myself and my loved ones.

I would say that a traditional Métis path is a hybrid of Christianity and Native Spirituality but these days a Métis person could be Wiccan, Buddhist or even a Druid. For many years my path was the spiritual path of my mother which was a blending of bits of Catholicism and the beliefs of our native ancestors but as with anything in our lives there comes change and if spirituality teaches us anything it is to look within ourselves for guidance.

Within this native woman sparkles an emerald green light, for years it huddled in a corner, waiting to be acknowledged, when I did a part of me smiled back at myself. From the ancestry of my English ancestors coupled with a vision from my own soul I found my spiritual balance. The ancestry of my Celtic side influenced my interest in the emerald path, the light of the Celtic Wheel glowed with an energy of wisdom that mesmerised my mind and illuminated my spirit. The Sabbats are spiritual markers that hold sacred energies, crossroads where I tap into ancient power and therefore become renewed and reinvigorated once again.

Who can explain the mind of the Creator? He is the maker of us all, so let's put away our assumptions of what a Pagan should be or what a Christian should be and promote the belief that the Creator loves diversity. As a mystic I hope to remove my mental restrictions that society ingrained within me and to experience spiritual evolution through personal revelations of the divine and see beyond the veil of dogma. Mysticism for me is about being in awe of this earthly journey, realising that the person who broke my heart is one of my greatest teachers and that after a rainfall a rainbow appears to remind me that the source of all life is faithful. My path as a mystic emphasises a sacredness for nature and a belief that there is a divine presence in all living things.

From my Celtic roots I have created rituals around the Celtic Wheel of the Year, passing through the eight celebrations I take time to pause and to reflect on the meaning of each sacred day. For myself it is this pausing; lighting my candles, making my offerings that reminds me of the progression of my earthly passage and my connection to the natural world. My spiritual growth is related to the cycles of the seasons as well as my experiences and challenges. Mother earth with her animals, plants and places becomes sacred and are given special meanings, nature teaches me many lessons.

Silence and surrender brings harmony to my mind and spirit and it is this attitude towards life that allows me to have inner peace. My life as a mystic is a love affair with God and Mother Earth. Walking in nature is one of my favourite things to do and this allows me to take time to pray and to connect with the divine.

Brisk fall days decorated with the enchanting colours of autumn herald the coming of the equinox. Mabon brings aromas that clear the heart and mind; with change comes realisations that urge me to transform with the landscape. I am changed by the power of creation, cooler days keep me indoors, it is also a signal that it is time to go within, to delve into the treasures of my soul, quiet reflections in natural surroundings increase my connection with my higher self. Autumn's glory is the glory of the Creator and while winter is lurking in the changeable days, mother earth's message is clear: prepare yourself for transformation.

Out of the darkness of winter comes spring with its message of hope and renewal. A heart shattered from pain embraces the meaning of Beltane; with arms outstretched to the Creator I am reminded of this precious gift of light and love.

It requires commitment from me to find the time to savour these pauses at the Sabbats. Often I find my life so busy with work and family that my devotional time can become neglected but what keeps me inspired is the beauty of nature. When I carve

out a moment to perform a ritual I do it not only as a demon-
stration of my belief in the divine but also for myself, these
moments are gifts that allow me to absorb the beauty of this
earth and of the energy of the Great Mystery ... the source of all
creation.

Through rituals and observing nature, I create harmony by
being harmonious with the spirit of creation. I believe that the
universe is a sentient being and everything contained within it
has purpose and is divinely fed. Plants, ancestors and animals
act as mediators between myself and the Creator. Communing
with all my relatives such as the cedar and the winged ones
creates a peaceful vibration and aids me in my understanding of
the world around me and the world within me. Taking time to
refresh and re-energise myself makes me a healthier person, I
find I can better handle the obligations I have to myself, my
family and my community.

The essence of spirituality is to know ourselves and be at
peace with our perception of the divine; we all search for inner
peace and happiness. No one's life is always smooth sailing and
often I need to be in touch with surroundings that are healing,
and that is nature.

The Sabbats forge my connection to Mother Earth and give
added meaning to the changing of the seasons. The four seasons
fill up the span of a year and there are four aspects of a human
being in the Medicine Wheel; the spiritual nature, the mental
nature, the emotional nature and the physical nature. I often find
myself examining one facet of myself as it oincides with the
season; not to say that I neglect the other sides to my nature but
it is sometimes necessary to reflect on a particular aspect of
myself and how my interconnection with others is going. Have I
been mindful of the needs of others or am I being self absorbed
and not seeing the hardships in others' lives?

Esbats – I am a lover of the moon; my heart always surrenders
to her pearlescent glow, white light being spread from above, so

soothing it banishes my stress and transforms my moods. It is a special time for me to connect with the energies of my ancestors, to pray for others and make offerings. During full moon I weave tender prayers of devotions to my ancestors, I cherish the wisdom of the Elders and I reflect on the dreams and visions they bestow on me.

When the weather is warm I love to sit beneath a willow tree and gaze up at Grandmother Moon. Amidst the peaceful tranquillity of a moonlit evening, I find the atmosphere conducive to enter into serious prayer and reflection. I adore the beauty of His creation; I offer my service to His divine plan for this world. No matter what our paths or lifestyles may be, I believe each of us has something to contribute to this world, I feel if we are caring people it is our obligation to contribute to our communities. We may have different backgrounds, cultures and beliefs but it is our differences that should urge us to reach out to another. Remember it is love that makes us consider the other person in ourselves.

I was born an empath and a clairvoyant; I feel the emotions of people and things even from a distance, life as an empath can be difficult. Growing up I felt bombarded with other people's feelings and symptoms of sickness, I have a heightened sensitivity to the world around me but in my connection with nature I find peace. One aspect of being empathic is that I do love being able to feel nature. It is this ability of sensing the feelings and personalities of Mother Earth's beings that makes life interesting and also inspires me to be spiritually green. I experience a heartfelt companionship with Mother Earth, I enjoy making the time to sit in a field and listen to the gentle breezes as they stroke my face, listening to the heartbeat of our mother. Being a clairvoyant is often overwhelming and that is why my quiet time is also my spiritual time. Standing under a dome of stars is a moment when all pressure stops; the peacefulness of the night allows me time to go within. Spirituality for me means being able to go within myself, to explore who I am and learn the meaning and purpose of my path.

I don't follow any organised religion or belong to a spiritual group, an experience in my twenties made me realise I did not want to be manipulated by someone else's belief in the divine. Religion to me is people's laws being passed down generation after generation and everyone believes it without questioning it and much of its power is the fear of damnation or a fear of being different. Religion can bind people together and it can tear them apart. I prefer the solitude of a mystic's path

For myself there must be a certain amount of searching and learning and then the striving must cease. At some point I knew it was time to just simply live in love and contemplation. I felt from the beginning of my spiritual journey that I didn't want to venture too far out of my own culture. I was aware of the depth of mystical traditions that existed within my own ancestors' beliefs and traditions and so I desired to explore their wisdom and see where that journey would take me.

Throughout the years the path that I have chosen has opened up for me as I have walked it. I didn't wake up at 17 years of age and think; gee I want to become a mystic. Realising I was a mystic actually took many years to discover.

In my initial stages of spiritual growth I was taught to smudge, pray, to come before the Creator with humbleness and an open heart. There is purity in simplicity, to be free of dogmatic beliefs and rules and just rest in the peaceful presence of the divine.

Unfortunately I ventured from my safe nest and briefly experimented with Christian Fundamentalism which was an extremely difficult experience and left me emotionally bankrupt and I returned to my childhood world beaten and spiritually wounded.

Time faded the pain but looking back I think it was Jesus who led me out of that situation; he was the calm in the hurricane.

Native spirituality is also my heritage, this way of life has no single founder or dogma, through ceremony and meditation my ancestors teach me that everything has being and deserves respect. Their wisdom and mastery sustain me, I cannot move forward wisely in my life without guidance from spirit. Listening to and reading mythical legends often has the ability to influence my life in a positive way. The blending of the mystical and the mundane in a manner that is grounding dissolves blockages and promotes healing.

Once I let go of fear and condemnation I began to grow spiritually through mysticism. I experienced a deeper realisation that my relationship with the Creator needs to be based on trust.

My childhood spirituality has greatly influenced my present spiritual beliefs and I find as I grow older I yearn to return to a spiritual path that I knew growing up. Going to Pow Wows, camping out, enjoying mom's fried bannock chased down with her sweet tea are some of my fondest memories and most spiritual ones.

I have been blessed that my Cree mother is a beautiful soul, the light that shines from her is pure and the path she taught me is an ancient one. Through ceremony I have these sudden moments of connection with the Creator in which I feel linked with the universe but do not pretend to completely understand the Divine in the twenty-first century, but I truly believe life is a holy contract we have with God, with Mother Earth and with each other.

Many of us including myself spend way too much time searching for meaning outside ourselves whereas there is no need to look any further than our own inner wisdom. If we feel insecure we look to others to validate us, if we are feeling drained we look to others to nourish us back to health. The flip side of the same coin is that we humans are not islands and we do need others but the key is balance. There is a difference in being alone and being lonely. What I have shared here is when I make time to be alone in prayer there is a serenity that fills me and learning who I am frees me from others' concepts of the Divine.

I don't always depend on others for my happiness. I know who I am, I can appreciate the beauty of solitude and the path of the mystic.

Like millions of others I realise our planet is in trouble. I do my best to contribute to tackling the challenges of our world by implementing practices such as recycling and buying items locally. I believe that if you have chosen a path that respects Mother Earth and honours all our relatives, then your lifestyle should reflect that choice. I live as a mystic, which means I strive to have that personal relationship with the Creator based on my own experiences, not controlled by someone else's opinion. Being spiritually green I strive each day to live in a ecologically friendly manner, my values are to be compassionate and loving to others and to the earth.

I try each day to avoid consumerist values and embrace more spiritual values, I pray and perform ceremony and even if it is only a few moments I can spare, I take time to connect with spirit. You may wonder why being spiritually green is so important to someone's life; I believe we are healthier in our minds and bodies when we flow with the natural rhythm of nature. Becoming quiet so we can hear the sound streams of Mother Earth and breathing in the scent of burning sage clears our minds and grounds us to the here and now. This grounding and clearing gives us balance so that we can live better lives. Each of us needs to live in harmony with each other and with the planet, material wealth is not the path to true happiness. Many of us myself included are learning this valuable lesson, I believe when we are working for a collective good for humanity and nature we can gain an inner satisfaction that our lives are taking on a deeper meaning. There is evidence throughout the world that spirituality was originally centred on our interaction with nature. I believe when spiritual beliefs see the Divine as immanent, people are more ecologically sensitive and responsible. With many people focused on environmental issues even mainstream religions have been encouraged to place an emphasis on living green.

Each day I try to pray and spend time outdoors, so that I can connect with the sacred. It is my opinion that people have both an ecological and spiritual connection to the Divine. My aim is to spread green spirituality beyond the borders of paganism and New Age religions. I hope that our common concern for the future of our environment can be a common ground between us and out of that will become a harmonious working relationship that will bridge past assumptions that each group has formed about the other.

Towards a Polytheist Psychology

Robin Herne

Academic psychology does not exist in a cultural void, but reflects the underlying values of the people researching or espousing a given theory. Perhaps the majority of modern theories as to the workings of the human mind are built upon a secular, arguably atheist bedrock that is prone to pathologize metaphysical experiences. This does not mean those theories are wrong, of course, but there has been a growing shift (albeit still a strangely secular one) to embrace the concept of multiple divinity as an active force within our psyches, exemplified by such writers as James Hillman.

For the purposes of this article, I'd like to push this envelope a little further and not view the Gods (and other beings) as neutered abstractions or somewhat literary templates exaggerating human characteristics. Rather, I'd like to explore the viability of an understanding of humanity that incorporates our relationships with entities that are acknowledged (by the theorist if few others) as real, independent sapient beings.

To some extent, a lot of the work has already been done by distant generations ~ those philosophers of the ancient world who first reflected on human nature and why people behave and think as they do.

Ancient Roman religion originated with the reverencing of *numina*, before their understanding of *deus* (Gods) became more personalised like that of the Greeks ~ though the Hellenics had the parallel notion of *daimones*. Each *numen* (the singular form of numina) embodied one concept, such as Pax (peace), Concordia (harmony), and Somnos (sleep). Exactly where a *numen* ends and *deus* begins is rather unclear, and may not have been considered important.

From what little is known of very early Celtic religion, their conception of deity may have been rather more akin to numina as well. One account describes the war lord Brennos being bemused by the tendency of the Greeks to depict their deities in human shape ~ presumably his culture saw them in more abstract, elemental terms. Many generations and a long distance later the Irish monk Tirechán recorded an encounter between two pagan women and St Patrick, in which Ethne asked the following questions of the bishop, *"Who is God and where is God and whose God is he and where is his dwelling-place? Has your God sons and daughters, gold and silver? Is he ever-living, is he beautiful, have many fostered his son, are his daughters dear and beautiful in the eyes of the men of the earth? Is he in the sky or in the earth or in the water, in rivers, in mountains, in valleys? Give us an account of him; how shall he be seen, how is he loved, how is he found, is he found in youth, in old age?"* Whilst these are words placed in the mouth of a pagan by a Christian scribe, they are nonetheless suggestive of how the later druidic pagans had come to see their deities to want to know if Jehovah was similar.

To the largely secular minds of twenty-first-century people, Roman numina appear as abstract nouns given vaguely mystical overtones. However, such a view lacks an understanding of how the ancients saw their divine presences.

Plato's famous Theory of Forms may well have been influenced by what he understood of the *daimones* of his own culture. He argued that the physical world was an emanation of a spiritual dimension wherein all things existed as perfect originals ~ both physical things (such as the Ideal Cow, Oak tree, Ruby etc.) and more abstract concepts (Ideal Love, Fear, Vengeance etc. ~ the numina Cupid, Pavor and Nemesis).

When the Romans spoke of the Pax they were not merely idealising transitory sensations of calm and imagining it as some sort of goddess. When Pax walks abroad the peace she visits on people is profound and transcendent. Similar might be said of all the other numina ~ that they go far beyond the individual, and that their presence cannot be confused with the brief experiences that in some sense contribute towards their being in the way that every raindrop contributes to the river (but could never be mistaken for it).

The distinction drawn above, between physical phenomena and mental ones, is a blurry one and sometimes rephrased as the separation between Gods of Nature and Gods of Civilisation ~ commentators on Heathenry often perceive this distinction between the Vanir and the Asgard deities.

It is blurry, if not actually false, for two reasons. Firstly, nothing that we class as abstract or mental is entirely so ~ we all know that anger, love etc. have biological ramifications in terms of increased heart rate, pupil dilation, diffusion of blood to surface capillaries, the release of certain neurotransmitters in the brain etc. It may equally be argued that few, if any, physical things are entirely physical for that matter. A chair is as much the manifestation of a carpenter's imagination as it is carved wood, and our understanding of other species and our love of categorising them again says as much about our brains' ability to process sensory information and allocate things to boxes (which exist more in our heads as schemata than in the things being allocated) as it does about objective reality.

Secondly, love may well be a human concept ... but aren't humans part of the natural world? As modern pagans we often unwittingly see the world in the dualistic terms evinced by two millennia of monotheism; we tend to think of humans as being somehow outside of nature. It is not uncommon to hear pagans objecting to aspects of human behaviour or thought as "unnatural".

If we humans can manifest romance, hatred, boredom, humour (which sidesteps the likelihood that other species also experience many of these abstract concepts), let alone dream up cities, computers and motorcars, then all these things are as much part of nature as storms or bird nests. Falling in love is as natural for humans as the urge to chase mice is for cats, likewise inventing tools, telling stories, and developing alphabets are all completely natural. The global spread of these habits in widely diverse groups of people demonstrates that.

Not wanting to sidestep the aforementioned issue entirely, few people who have lived with dogs for any prolonged period of time can doubt that they experience many of the same emotions and abstract mental states that we do. Nor are dogs the only species to have some or all of the same internal passions as humans. If species contemporary to humanity can have such psychological complexity, is there any real reason to suppose that at least some of the species inhabiting this planet prior to the evolution of humanity did not share at least some of that internal life too?

If that were the case then such numina are not as such the product of our human consciousness, but integral to consciousness in general ~ beyond the bounds of any single species. Human psychology then partakes of these transpersonal forces. We are used to thinking of ourselves as discrete entities, and often adopt an almost adolescent defensive petulance at the implication that someone else might (heaven forfend) under-stand how we feel or what we think.

What I wish to propose is that we are not isolated individuals, but rather that we have what might be termed permeable walls. This is an idea explored by others, including Jung with his concept of the Collective Unconscious through which the arche-types swim like vast, barely comprehendible cetaceans.

Rollo May grasped the idea which the ancients were au fait with, that when numina approach too closely they can sometimes overwhelm our individuality. The Greeks accepted that a person in the grip of Eros fell madly in love ~ the loss of sanity being far from some Mills and Boon lovey-dovey romance. That temporary madness could lead to erotic obsession with the most inappropriate individuals (Pasiphae lusting after a bull, Phaedra fixating on her stepson etc.), or people carrying out unhinged acts in a bid to win their beloved's attentions. For the Greeks the hope was that Eros would move on quickly and the madness would subside to a healthier, gentler affection for an appropriate target.

Sexual obsession is as common now as it was in the distant past, as are other forms of numinous possession ~ people so consumed by a single mental state (anger, jealousy and despair being amongst the commonest) that any form of balance is temporarily lost.

Such visitations from external forces were sometimes regarded as a natural consequence of the individual's actions, unwitting or otherwise. Phaedra was driven mad because her stepson Hippolytus had shunned the altars of Eros' mother, Aphrodite. There are two important insights into psychology to derive from this myth: firstly, to deny an aspect of the universe (both the actual goddess but also the areas of life she articulates herself through, namely love and sexuality) is deeply unhealthy and leads to imbalance. Within polytheism the Gods must be acknowledged, either formally through ritual and offerings, or casually by attending to their areas of life both in our behaviours and our internalised states (referring back to the earlier point that nothing is entirely external nor internal). Or by combining both routes of course. Secondly, we exist collectively.

Virginia Sapir made ground breaking work establishing ~ or perhaps re-establishing a long-ignored truth ~ the concept of the family nexus and family therapy. Though a time consuming and expensive form of therapy, this approach acknowledges that none of us are islands developing in isolation from one another. We are constantly influencing and being influenced by the people around us.

To push a step further, this collective psychology is not restricted to the nuclear family but expands to the wider communities in which we live.

Hippolytus caused the offence but it was Phaedra who became mad, Eros driving her to tear her stepson's life apart. Our barriers are permeable, other people can begin manifesting effects (destructive or beneficial) that originate from something we have done, and likewise we can become the unwitting actors in someone else's ritual drama.

Whilst on the theme of permeability, it's worth considering that not only are there many gods, but there are many selves. We are encouraged to think of ourselves as singular beings, but as John Rowan pointed out in his sub-personality thesis, we have many overlapping identities. The notion of situational identities is nothing new and we are all at least vaguely aware that Mr Jones at work is James to his wife, Dad to his children, Jimbo to his rugby mates, Jimmy to his dotty Great Aunt, and possibly Maureen of a Thursday night when his wife is down the bingo and wondering why her knicker elastic never lasts a week. Not only does each identity have its own name, but often its own manner of dress, own lexical range etc. In most people for most of the time (I'm assuming) these selves work in reasonable harmony with each other. However, we have probably all experienced periods when the ambitions of our working selves conflict with the nurturing instincts of our parenting selves or the pleasures of our social selves.

What I'm suggesting goes beyond the adoption of different roles ~ though clearly these different selves evolve in partial response to external demands ~ and into the realms of semi-autonomous beings sharing the same body, each with their own burgeoning, and sometimes overtly distinctive, identities.

If asked which was the "real" him, James Jones might reply differently at varied stages in his life. In a sense the question is misleading, because they are all the real him because James Jones in a gestalt of all those selves ... and not simply the selves that operate now, but also those selves that may have been discarded in childhood or adolescence, and those selves that may not yet emerge for another 20 or 30 years.

Most people are quite aware of the different identities contained within them, only a tiny number of people sharding (mainly as a result of severe psychological trauma) to the point where they sometimes black out and do things that other identities allegedly have no recollection of. Or where, arguably, the voices and opinions of one or more selves seems utterly external to other selves, and feel like outside voices.

Not only are we a "pantheon" of psychological identities, but we are also a biological gestalt that stays alive because of the assorted bacteria living within us. Like trees, we support a host of other life forms within our beings.

Coming back to an earlier aside, monotheists and atheists often find it humorous that polytheists have a deity for everything ~ including sewers (Cloacina) and homosexuality (Tu Er Shen). It strikes me as dazzling common sense to embrace every single thing, be that the shit-sodden tunnels that save countless people from diphtheria and Hepatitis A, or a form of human behaviour that many mainstream religions denigrate and persecute despite the fulfilment it has brought to countless lives. This involved form of animism is the recognition that all things are sacred, and that in a healthy society a place is found for everything. The implications of this are far reaching, more than can be reasonably explored in a short chapter.

A society that represses a subgroup frequently also encourages most or all of its members to repress some part of their own psyches, to leave one of their altars untended. Doing this almost guarantees that not only will the excluded group seek ways to rise up and lash back, but that the un-honoured deities will send their numina to cause mayhem.

Modern pagans talk a great deal about venerating Nature, by which we usually mean forests, mountains and wild creatures. Whilst we should certainly be doing all that, I am extending this veneration to include the honouring of our own human nature.

What does it mean to be human? How can we most effectively allow our humanity to flower?

Talking about the flowering of humanity is perhaps a tad misleading, because it implies something fragrant and joyful. If we open to human nature then we have to include the odious side as well as the noble one. Instead of seeking to sublimate or relinquish anger, we may be better off trying to find ways for people to vent their rage in manageable ways; likewise our greed, cruelty, laziness and so forth.

In looking at what makes us human, I am inclined to agree with Martin Rowson that it is not so much that we have anything utterly unique that distinguishes us from other creatures, but rather that we take a number of traits to far greater heights (or depths, as the case may be) than other species do. So rather than try to draw up a list of what humans do that no other creature on Earth does, let's just think of a few traits common to every known culture in every known time period.

Humour in all its varied forms is a constant, as is animism ~ which Piaget saw as an infantile stage that we mature out of, but rather I suggest it is basically the default setting of the human mind, to perceive (not imagine) that we are surrounded by living, sapient beings that we can interact with. Storytelling, music, language, tool use, home building, psychedelic substance use, keeping pets, decorative arts, and the urge to dance are but a few of the worldwide habits that we humans exhibit. Not every single person wants to dance or enjoys the company of pets, but as a species we repeatedly demonstrate these behaviours and develop them to a very involved degree. A religious or political elite that attempts to ban people from singing, speaking, or consuming alcohol is, I suggest, trying to force humans to be less than human ~ no matter how much they may claim they are attempting to improve or refine our natures.

Whilst other religions may exhort people give up this or sublimate that, polytheist traditions embrace the full range of what it means to be human ~ the good, the bad and the peculiar. If the fate of Hippolytus tells us anything then it is that we should leave at least some sort of offering at every altar in the temple of our psyches ~ and that to devote ourselves to one altar, one self to the exclusion of all others, is a deeply unhealthy and fraught path to tread.

The later Roman perception of a *deus* was, in art at least, very humanised. However, a clearer distinction between numina and *deus* may not be the issue of human representation, but that numina have a singular focus whilst gods are complex entities with a multitude of traits, passions, and agendas. Humanity, perhaps, is more akin to numina, given our capacity for monomaniacal obsessions and tendency to allow one mental state to overwhelm us through addictive cravings, depression, monstrously ruthless ambition etc. A number of religions over the ages have encouraged their devotees to become like Gods ~ and in this I can but concur, for we are best advised to grow more branches and, like any vast and ancient tree, allow more beings to dwell within us.

We are at our best when we flower in complexity.

After Paganism

Emma Restall Orr

For over twenty-five years I thought of myself as a British Pagan.

The definition of Pagan I used was simple, and perhaps that simplicity allowed me to retain the word. For me, a Pagan is one who looks primarily to the lore of nature, not to the laws of man, there finding the teachings and guidance necessary to live an honourable, sustainable and peaceful existence.

To add a little more colour to the definition, as a Pagan my own religious practice has been fundamentally animistic, where, pantheistically, god is nature, and, polytheistically, nature is the gathering of countless gods. There is nothing supernatural, nothing beyond nature: the word encompasses all that is. Every atom, every cell, every whisper of thought, every gust of wind, is a part of nature's soul, of nature's mind, of the entirety that is god. As such, nature is sacred, as is every part of nature, every creature that makes up the whole of nature. Furthermore, being integral to each moment of nature's existence, everything thus exists with equal value within nature.

For me, such a perspective calls for a very gentle way of living. The presence of any human being has a heavy impact on the environment, after all: we take, use, adapt, consume, just to survive. If we are to perceive nature as sacred, care, thought and consideration must be taken with each and every decision, weighing up what is truly needed, what will cause unnecessary harm, what will contribute positively and what will not. It is not an easy path to take, but it is, for me, Paganism.

There have been times when, in very conventional societies, I have been cautious about referring to myself as a Pagan. Although much has changed in the last two or three decades, there are still pockets of conservative England where the word is not broadly understood, and to use it out of place would provoke more confusion than clarity. There have been times too when I have been proud to use the label openly. Stepping forward and articulating my beliefs in public, I have been glad of the opportunities I have had to take an active part in lifting the ignorance. Asserting and explaining my perspective, I have been able to offer my enthusiasm, and in doing so perhaps to inspire others to find their own spiritual truths, and to grasp the courage they needed to be able to express them.

However, there have also been many times when I have been deeply embarrassed to be known as a Pagan. From correspondence and conversations I have had over the years, I know I speak for many when I say that I have sometimes felt a heart-sinking, sickening confusion that has led me to wonder whether I could ever call myself Pagan again.

Here are two images that I find difficult. A group of Pagans sit in a fast food joint, overweight but nevertheless eating cheap meat and other heavily processed foods, wearing sweatshop-made clothes, whilst bitching about other Pagans in the community. Out of the city a gathering of Pagans drifts away from an old stone circle where they have left not only cigarette stubs and beer cans, but candles and other non-biodegradable offerings that are no more than litter.

A further image may feel more subtle. A group of Pagans stand in a woodland glade at night, reading the scripts of their ritual by the light of electric torches, blinded to the stars above let alone the ecosystem through which they have so clumsily processed. To make it worse, perhaps they have cast their ritual circle with salt, and invoked gods of lands many thousands of miles away while paying no heed to the spirits of the landscape within which they stand.

Now and then I have wondered over the past five years whether it is getting better. An increasing number of Pagans do appear to be vocalising their thoughts about ethical behaviour, thinking about their impact on the environment, acting with respect towards other religious traditions and cultures. Then something erupts on Facebook, and within minutes every twenty-first-century medium of gossip is flooded while some high priestess or arch druid pours the burning oil of vitriol over another hapless individual or organisation who has in some way upset them.

This is not what I understand to be Paganism.

The problems, of course, are inherent to our human nature. In every human society, in families and voluntary groups, places of work and places of worship, we encounter blinkered actions based on ignorance, and power-plays based on insecurities. What interests me, and concerns me, is whether there are elements within modern Paganism that encourage such very poor behaviour.

In most Pagan traditions, the *individual* is considered central to his own world and to his own religious understanding. To begin with, the priest is not an indispensable medium between the people and the gods: more often his or her role is that of a facilitator or teacher, encouraging each person to discover their own particular and intimate experience of the divine. Where this works, it removes a hierarchy within ritual groups, allowing for an equality and respect that is a valuable characteristic of Paganism.

This emphasis on the individual can be seen throughout Pagan traditions. Seeking visions or insight, looking perhaps to understand the patterns of creation and chaos, or seeking to hone his own wit and will, the Pagan strives to learn how to discipline his mind. Self reflection and self development are crucial to many Pagan paths; these teachings guide the student to find a strong sense of his own empowerment. Through cleansing the self, many strive for what they believe to be an enlightened state, where the self feels as if it were filled with love and light. The aim or side-effect of many Pagan rituals is the generation of energy, through dance, rhythm, chanting, and the like, which in turn can provoke an exhilarated and heightened awareness of the self. Indeed, most Pagan rituals and gatherings are rich with sensuality, the individual's tangible experiences being thoroughly encouraged: feasting, alcohol, music, dance, drugs, sexuality, and all kinds of tactile creative arts are explored and celebrated. Even within the most cerebral practices, visceral sensations are often a measure of efficacy.

All these are a part of what makes Paganism so deliciously substantial and earthy, and so accessible for those who are uncomfortable in a more conventional or conformist cultural setting. With its roots deep in the soil of landscape, in the blood of ancestry, it is these very Pagan attitudes towards the experience of individuality that can be seen as the defining marks of a nature-based religion.

So where is the problem?

The majority of religious and spiritual traditions will affirm that it is valuable, even necessary, to begin the journey by finding a sense of oneself, or one's self. For the individual who has been broken by abuse or trauma, a damaged sense of who they actually are can lead to relationship crises, so perpetuating the abuse or isolation. The simple lack of gentleness within a dysfunctional and uncaring society can leave a person with no coherent or positive identity, and so no sense of value for themselves or anything else. Only once we have found that initial sense of self is it possible for the self to grow, finding confidence, and in time perhaps the stillness and certainty of peace. Any caring religious community will guide its adherents towards such a goal.

Paganism focuses from the outset on this search for the self. However, in most Pagan teachings, this appears as the be-all and end-all, the ultimate goal. The authentic self is sought and, through ritual, meditation and community interaction, that search continues until it is found nestled within the fabric of nature, affirmed (for the lucky ones) by a group of caring and creative individuals, and there celebrated as a valid expression of individuality. All the person need then do is devise a sound way of living which that same group will support and applaud.

But human nature is flawed. The human capacity for self-awareness is complex. While it does provide us with a sense of who we are, during hard times it can lead us to doubt ourselves and crumble, losing confidence in who it is we think we are. Yet it is also what draws confidence back in once more, helping us to recover and re-create a sense of self, a process which we go through again and again from early childhood and indeed through most of our lives. Establishing its stronghold at the centre of our being, it is from there that this self-awareness declares itself the *I*.

This human *I*, our conscious centre or ego, is such a crucial part of what makes us human. It fuels and enables our striving, growing, changing, learning. Every experience, every idea, every flood of sensation, adds to that sense of self and its ego, allowing us to feel confident in its various statements of *I am*. As such, the ego has a keen sense of its own need to survive. Much of the work it does is the jostling for and affirming of its position within a community. With positive creativity, this assertive ego finds a position of leadership in order to improve conditions for others. However, all too often, the self-importance of the *I* takes over, the insecure ego working solely to benefit itself.

Witnessing the bitching and gossiping in the Pagan community, given its focus on personal empowerment and celebration of the self, I am concerned that this is a set of traditions which is at risk of nurturing self-importance.

Of course, some readers may justifiably dismiss my words as invalid criticism of their own Pagan tradition, on the basis that what I am commenting on are purely the simpler and overt teachings. Some Pagan paths do have mystical, occult or contemplative grades, with principles that delve right under the ego.

However, the fact that the vast majority do not reach these levels of training or understanding only supports my concerns.

It is relevant that I touch on some of these deeper teachings in this essay, sharing a little of their place in my own beliefs and practice. Before I do so, however, I would like to consider another pertinent aspect of Paganism that further adds to my concern.

Our capacity for complex language is another human quality that I think both helps and hinders our religious exploration and our striving for peace. While allowing us the benefit of subtle and specific communication, each word is also a limitation. With a freshly picked raspberry in the hand, we can drench our senses with its scent, colour, form, texture and taste; on the other hand, the word *raspberry* alludes to those qualities, together with perhaps dozens of other personal memories and associations, but it is no more than an abstraction. The experience of being utterly in love is one that both fills and empties us, leaving us trembling with urgency, hope, bliss and despair, but these words with which I have described it are but a faint and brief reflection of the actual feelings themselves.

In Paganism, despite so many strands of its practice being grounded in the tenets of a nature-based religion, there are an alarming number of abstractions, a good number of which are religious and ritual elements so poorly taught that they have become abstractions. For example, words such as spirit and soul are seldom given any defined meaning, and as such allow invocations and prayers based upon them to meander with no focused aim.

Furthermore, for a good number in Pagan traditions, gods are no longer externally existent forces or entities within nature, but merely constructs of the human psyche. Together with angels, demons and elementals, as archetypes they may be described by some as hovering within the collective human unconscious, but still they are abstractions. It is no wonder that many give up on gods as actual beings when they have chosen to work with a goddess or god simply because they like the list of associations that go with it. Motherhood, fertility, the wildwood, strength, wizardry, whatever it may be, we are encouraged when we find others who can confirm that Cernunnos or Hecate is what we believe him or her to be. But these are ideas, found in books and shared with other people. They are not the gods that we encounter when the river banks burst, or the buds on the apple tree eventually break open, or when we are screaming with pain.

Equally, when prayers are made to the ancestors, all too often the individual is happy to disregard his parents, perhaps his grand- and great-grandparents, and any other flawed human beings either alive or within living memory, reaching instead to an abstract notion of ancient ancestors, who are no more than an idea of tribal coherence, warrior-like pride and rural wisdom, or some such perfect archetype.

It is not possible to make a relationship with an abstraction. As ideas within our own minds, when we call to the spirits of the north, or some goddess we've read about, we are reaching simply to some storehouse of memory, reminding our selves of what we know, listing again the associations we have learned. That may indeed evoke a sensation of change, but that effect is not externally sourced.

To be in company with Pagans whose *relationships* with their gods and ancestors are evident, who are communicating with other entities within nature's mind instead of talking to themselves, is a true delight. Such Pagans, I believe, are in a small minority, however. Why this is so, I would suggest, is once again the over-emphasis on, and the complacent acceptance of, the individual self.

If we were to consider teachings that take a seeker through and beyond the self, there are a number of routes we could take in Paganism. Needless to say, whichever I were to choose here, offering a sketch in this essay would be to risk a few fundamental complications. Perhaps most crucially, as we go deeper, language becomes increasingly less effective, leaving us with yet more abstractions, and as a result personal experience becomes the only key to understanding. Without that experience, the words are inevitably meaningless or misconstrued.

Nonetheless, and given the added limit of a thousand words, I shall offer a few ideas.

Fully engaging with the teachings of any spiritual or religious path is a harrowing journey, and one that does not take the traveller simply from A to B. Labyrinthine, the path winds backwards and forwards, allowing us to progress most painfully slowly, with bursts of glorious insight and heavy slumps of regression. It is a journey that requires us to submit completely to the indignity of learning, being willing to struggle, to flounder and fall, to suffer, breaking ourselves apart. Only then can the processes of fundamental change occur, reconfiguring us as it does way beneath the levels at which we can reason and control. Losing the certainties of our assumptions, moving through the darkness of not knowing, feeling no stability under foot, we find ourselves at last on the painful path of awakening.

A minority are compelled to take themselves to this edge, seeking it out of their own volition. Desperate to release themselves from the meaningless tedium of mundane living, filled with the desire to understand the very essence of being, they hurl themselves into situations of crisis and strife, using drugs, fasting, pain, and other physical and emotional stresses that shake up the hidden and habitual patterns deep within. Such pro-active steps usually last a matter of hours, days or weeks, no more, but a few find the inner gateways to what St John of the Cross called 'the long dark night of the soul', and there they wander through months or years of doubt and despair, in search of faith, insight, or revelation.

But most healthy human beings cannot voluntarily head out to the brink: a natural survival instinct kicks in to prevent such self-sabotage, an internal sense protecting us from situations where the ego is under threat, where the *I am* will be humiliated by the brutality of truth and failure. The majority, then, who end up walking the long dark roads of suffering have been pushed there - by illness, trauma or depression.

Whether they have sought out such difficulties or been pushed into them by fate, many speak of encounters there with the forces of darkness. Some describe or experience them as evil but, to those eager to learn, these are nature's most potent teachers: the dark gods. Without them it would be impossible to change. They are the power of formlessness, and to face them is to be touched by that power. Our spiritual challenge is to allow that power to deconstruct, to destroy, to demolish, not knowing what the consequences will be.

Some remain overwhelmed by that darkness, the survival instinct petering out, the years sliding by in numbness, confusion and regret. For a good number, however, there does come a turning point, inspired perhaps by some small act of kindness or serendipity at just the right moment in time, and the experience of anguish begins to transform, becoming instead one of profound learning. When at last such individuals return to the world, functional once more, the pain has made them stronger, and many face life with a new zeal to make it worthwhile. Re-establishing its centre, the *I* wakes, as if a grey veil has been lifted, its view of the world changed, cleansed by the process. Indeed, through the sloughing off of the old self, a sense of *being a part of* something bigger is often newly felt, bringing an exquisite sense of connection. And with that feeling often comes a rush of bliss - a sort of broad and unconditional love - which marks a rebirth into a spiritually meaningful life, fuelled by a new empathy and care.

Although such journeys can be extraordinarily profound, their effects seldom last a lifetime. The fuel burns hard and fast, inspiring the individual to express that exhilaration openly, finding ways of giving, sharing, healing, changing the world around them. But after weeks, months, maybe years, it burns out, the power of the transformation wearing off. The self at the centre, the subjective experience of being, the *I*, once more strengthened by the daily actions of living. The sense of connection may persist for some using regular religious or spiritual practice, but the majority slide back into lives where the ego begins again to jostle for position.

Where the suffering and transformation has allowed the emergence of a spiritual teacher, whose subsequent work has nourished his ego to the point of bloating, we find the New Age gurus, and the high priestesses and arch druids of the Pagan community, who are the most dangerous. For they are teachers whose experiences have clearly provided them with some depth and understanding, but whose self-importance will provoke them to use their inner strength in truly vicious ways to protect that sense of self.

A minority never *return* from that long dark period of suffering, yet nor do they remain in its grip. For these, the hardship has broken the ego so completely it simply cannot reform. The centre is gone, leaving a darkness, an empty hole, a void of unknowing. The person is still there, as a scaffold of memory around that dark hollow, but what steps back into the world is the coherence of a self with no centre, no ego, no drive to be someone, no need for certainty, indeed no personal need to be alive at all.

With the loss of the ego, we lose the sense of separation enough to feel fully a part of an environment, to achieve that blissful state of connection, but the *I* remains sufficiently intact to savour that bliss. When the centre is gone, however, there is no *I am* to be inspired by the experience. The individual self is a functional tool, but there is no experience of its individuality. Around the empty core is, instead, a being who exists in a state of integration. The environment, the context of its being - nature

- is at every moment a weave of bliss and pain, of suffering and inspiration, of ease and effort: inhalation and exhalation. Nothing is special. Everything is ordinary. And utterly sacred.

Devoid of the drama of the ego, and without the individuated emotional experience of *I am* (- I am miserable, in pain, depressed, joyful, blissed out), it is this state that is the long slow path of growing selflessness. The work of living continues to be done, the caring, sharing, giving work of a worthwhile life, but it is not fuelled by obligation, nor by the exhilaration of empathy, nor any sense of spiritual connection: life continues because of and through the simple integrity of nature.

Through the period of suffering we may have faced the dark gods, but here we breathe them and are breathed by them. They live within us. Yet we are no longer afraid, or fighting them, striving to retain some form of being. It is not an encounter, but an assimilation: an integration. And with that comes the deepest possible peace.

When I have spoken a little of such teachings elsewhere, others have responded with the riposte that what I am referring to is not British Paganism, but an intrusion of Eastern ideas. Contradicting my words, the critics assert the importance of the authentic and uninhibited self, and the celebration of that self, its experiences and creativity, as being central to the Western tradition. My perspective is described as a dangerous trend towards negation, with its inevitable resulting slide towards the devaluing of personal freedom.

Such words provoke me once again to question whether I am a Pagan.

As an animist, my metaphysics states that all nature is awake with awareness, with the capacity for experience and response. Consciousness, in its inconceivably broad diversity of being, is present as the tiniest particles and as its universal completeness, and every configuration in between: cells and supernovas, memories and mountains, brainwaves and snowflakes.

Pantheistically, then, I perceive nature as a divine whole, a fabric in the perpetual process of creativity. Nature is integration as god.

As a religious person, my search is for god. I strive to experience the wholeness of god and, understanding all of nature to be sacred with divinity, my wish is to live in peace with every part of god as nature. In order to do that, I must breathe with the dark gods until my self is released, softly and irrevocably dissolved into that sacred breath, that my being may fully awake to the natural integration that is god.

Within myself, I feel this to be Paganism.

However, for the time being, I am still in doubt as to whether or not to refer to myself as a Pagan.

MOON
BOOKS

Moon Books invites you to begin or deepen your encounter with
Paganism, in all its rich, creative, flourishing forms.